The US
CONSTITUTION
of 1791

and the

Fugitive Slave Clause

Other books by Norman Coles

John Ashton's Case for James II (Edwin Mellen Press, 1998)

Human Nature and Human Values (Egerton Press, available via Amazon, 2004)

Interpreting Politics in the USA (Sussex Academic Press, 2009)

The US CONSTITUTION of 1791

and the

Fugitive Slave Clause

A Philosophical Re-rendering of
Legislative Authority
Ambiguities and Conflicts

Norman Coles

sussex
ACADEMIC
PRESS
Brighton • Chicago • Toronto

2 4 6 8 10 9 7 5 3 1

First published in 2020 by
SUSSEX ACADEMIC PRESS
PO Box 139
Eastbourne BN24 9BP

Distributed in North America by
SUSSEX ACADEMIC PRESS
Independent Publishers Group
814 N. Franklin Street
Chicago, IL 60610

British Library Cataloguing in Publication Data
A CIP catalogue record for this book is available from the British Library.

Library of Congress Cataloging-in-Publication Data
To be applied for.

Paperback ISBN 978-1-78976-042-2

Typeset & designed by Sussex Academic Press, Brighton & Eastbourne.
Printed by TJ International, Padstow, Cornwall.

Contents

"One day Frances stopped the carriage to converse with an old blind slave woman, who was at work 'turning the ponderous wheel of a machine' in the yard. The work was hard but she had to do something she explained 'and this is all I can do, now I am so old'. When Frances asked about her family she revealed that her husband and all her children had been sold long ago to different owners and she had never heard from any of them again. This sad encounter left a lasting impression on Frances . . . "

"A few days afterwards the Sewards came across a group of slave children chained together on the road outside Richmond, Henry described the sorrowful scene:

'Ten naked little boys between six and twelve years old, tied together, two by two, by their wrists were all fastened to a long rope and followed by a tall gaunt white man who, with his long lash, whipped up the sad and weary little procession, drove it to the horse trough to drink and thence to a shed where they sobbed and moaned themselves to sleep'. The children had been purchased from different plantations that day and were on their way to be auctioned off at Richmond."

"Frances could not bear to continue her journey. 'Sick of slavery and the South' she wrote in her diary; 'the evil effects coming constantly before me and marring everything'."

From *Team of Rivals,* by Doris Kearns Goodwin
(Penguin Books, 2009; Chapter 3, page 79, paras. 2, 3 and 4)

'Cassivellaunus, the King of the Britons, sends his greetings to Gaius Julius Caesar. The Cupidity of the Roman people, my deal Caesar, is really quite beyond belief. They have an insatiable thirst for anything made of gold or silver, to the point that they cannot even leave us alone, although we live over the edge of the world and far beyond the perilous seas. They even have the nerve to stretch out their greedy hands towards our small revenues which, up to now, we have enjoyed in peace. This does not satisfy them: they want us to surrender our liberty and to endure perpetual bondage by becoming subject to them . . .

It is friendship you should have asked of us, not slavery. For our part we are more used to making allies than to enduring the yoke of bondage. We have become so accustomed to the concept of liberty that we are completely ignorant of what is meant by submitting to slavery . . .'

From *The History of the Kings of Britain* by Geoffrey of Monmouth

A saying of John Hollow Horn (of his people: *The Oglala Lakota*, given by James Wilson as a motto for his book: *The Earth Shall Weep* [Picador, 1998]). This saying applies also to the fate of people enslaved.
'Some day the earth will weep;
she will beg for her life, she will cry with tears.'

Dedication

To those millions torn by slave-hunters from home, mother, father, sisters and brothers, marched under an unrelenting sun hundreds of miles, chained then or later, thrown into prison, then compelled to a slave-hold more smelly, crowded and tortuous than an ant-heap. Then again chained, then put on a block and sold, then held as property, then perhaps lashed and put to a lifetime of hard labor; then perhaps sold again, parted from husbands, wives, children, then forced to labor in old age and then to die.

May words always preserve their memory as individual and their inalienable human dignity – though words can recreate only a small part of their sufferings.

AIMS

The times with which this book is concerned were truly terrible ones for slaves. They were hard ones for opponents of slavery especially in the United States. Public opinion alone could act as a tyrannical force. It might well have dented and changed the words in which I now condemn slavery had I lived then. I doubtless would have been less brave than those who risked their lives then, when even a mild expression of Abolitionism provoked often brutal bodily harm!

But, as Bishop Butler reminded us, each thing is what it is and not another. Slavery is property in human flesh, Geoffrey de Ste Crux tells us that the cruelty is so refined that (some) slaves are brutalised, not by mere ownership by another, but by the powers associated with a right of ownership being exercised over them by some agent (e.g. of another), who enforces rules with whips and stick. The slave is caught in a kind of Catch 22! His or her rights as humans are in effect traded – without his or her consent – to give another total power over him or her . . . That is devilish and inhuman.

I have tried in this book, as a philosopher, to show many points of conflict and plain contradictions between the 1791 Constitution of the United States and:

(a) chattel slavery in US States;

(b) the view that there was in the 1791 Constitution Federal Authority to (violently) 'deliver up' 'escaped' slaves to their 'owners'. The authority was supposed to derive from paragraph 3 of Section 2 of Article IV of the Constitution. But I show that this paragraph did not mention, specify or refer to slaves at all!; and

(c) already by 1840 the great Abolitionist lawyer Alvan Stewart had proved good legal reasons for Abolition.

I use both logic and history to show these points.

Acknowledgements

I thank and acknowledge all the people mentioned here for their help. This was of various kinds. They are the source of some of my lines of thought. But in no case are they responsible for my own arguments – and they may not agree with many. I may have made mistakes either of fact or logic. (For instance, many scholars will disagree with my many criticisms of Washington – and the wide scope I give to almost all the rights in The Bill of Rights).

My wife, Janet, and my friends Ian Shanks, Mike Punter, Patrick Glass and Jim Jefferies discussed many points with me. I owe them very much.

I am very grateful for very much hospitality at Cornell to Professor David Lyons and his wife – however this book occurred very much later (a quarter of a century) – and readers – as I do – will see that it has not had the great benefit of his meticulous and illuminating philosophical and legal scholarship and critique.

Professors Robert Natelson and Andre Meyer and Richard Creel wrote to me with answers to some questions – but may not agree with some or all of my views. I am very grateful to these distinguished scholars – and also to my friend – just as distinguished – of fifty years, Dr Timothy Potts, who provided a wholly new field of reference (to Fr J. F. Maxwell's book detailed in *Authorities*). Also Ted Polyhemus for data on the history of slavery in New Jersey. My friend, Dr Miriam Griffin put me in touch with Professor Natelson and I thank them both deeply. Again, neither are responsible for any of my mistakes. Professor Hugh Brogan answered one query for me.

Finally, I should thank the readers of this book. They will meet with arguments that are quite different in many ways from those in most works on the US Constitution(s) and US slavery! I ask them to be especially critical of my reasoning – since, as far as I know, not many scholars would dismiss 'The Fugitive Slave Clause' as completely and

ACKNOWLEDGEMENTS

utterly as I do – holding it never in any way mentioned slaves! Nor – I argue – did it give any authority to 'deliver up' fugitive slaves.

Alvan Stewart, the great Abolitionist lawyer, [as his work is presented by Professor Jacobus Ten Broek in *Equal Under Law* (Collier Books, New York, 1965)], was an early champion of the antithesis of the US Bill of Rights to slavery. His work – and that of other early Abolitionists (Henry Highland Garnett for one) – remains as relevant, brave and far-seeing as ever. Had they been heeded US slavery (in US States) could have been decisively proved as Unconstitutional as early as 1838!

NORMAN COLES
(Hastings, Easter 2019)

Preface

Like many people in many countries I was drawn by the wisdom and genius of Abraham Lincoln to study parts of American history. Initially I read about Lincoln's childhood, his early life and early career and then his career a few years later. At that point I'd not read much about Lincoln's later career and the Civil War years – though American friends did direct me to articles on the Civil War.

After some years of this reading I was aware of Lincoln's (undue) reverence for Washington. He rightly revered the (1788 and 1791) Constitution(s). Then I read Robert Harvey's vigorous (and very debatable), masterpiece on the years before, during (and after) The War of Independence *(A Few Bloody Noses)* and also Esmond Wright's earlier book *Washington and the American Revolution* (Penguin, 1973). Then a book which gave a fuller American perspective Clinton Rossiter: *The First American Revolution* (Harvest, 1956). Harvey and Rossiter were especially incisive in examining causes of American thought – though they disagreed about Britain's role.

I did not agree with all Harvey's judgements (in particular, it seemed to me that British policy pre-1775 had been far too lenient in regard to the evil of slavery and too adverse to Colonial interests in trade matters), but his masterly control of narrative and detail made me think very, very hard about the formation of Congress and the (1788 and 1791) Constitutions. But I still had not read clear and detailed narratives of Lincoln's later career and the Civil War years. So I then read many fuller biographies of Lincoln and numerous books on all aspects of the Civil War [by Shelby Foote and James McPherson (for example)]. This involved detailed study of both Generals Lee and Grant.

In time I had the good fortune, additionally, to find a masterpiece on all topics, *Team of Rivals* by Doris Kearns Goodwin (Penguin Books, Great Britain, 2009), a book now very well known throughout the world. This gave full and masterly treatment, not only of Lincoln's life, ideas, and ordeals at this period (from his election as President to his assassination), and of those of his main Cabinet colleagues – William Seward and Salmon Chase). The book also gave insights into the thinking of some Civil War Generals. It also exposed much Southern prejudice and violence (of Preston Brooks against Charles Sumner for instance).

All these books gradually – but inexorably – led me to the question – why did so many Americans from 1770 on, want Independence from Britain but to retain slavery? Lord Acton contends that it was mainly because they thought a British tyranny would come. Robert Harvey – by contrast – points to many past frictions between British troops and American militias. Gary Nash and Clinton Rossiter pinpoint many kinds of previous class – antagonisms against the 'gentry' order and show there was an environment very favourable to freedom [though not to prosperity – (but Robert Harvey thinks prosperity was general)]. Harvey and Rossiter (and many other historians), point to the simple fact that many Americans wanted (to keep) slaves. All these (and other reasons), have some role in explanation – but do they fully explain the fact that the 1788 (and then the 1791) US Constitution was held and interpreted (generally) as sanctioning US slavery even though among its aims was justice? Also liberty!! Also domestic peace! Here was a deep paradox – that needed more study – and studies. Justice, liberty (and peace) required no slaves – why then have US slavery?

I think a causal factor in early American troubles was an undue respect for Washington and a very widespread failure to distinguish free, independent action from social liberty. Independence made possible a wider field of (free) independent action for citizens (of the USA) – but it by no means made prevalent social liberty. This would have required (at least) freedom of work and movement for most US residents, (not criminals of course – who might be jailed). Jefferson may have seen this distinction, but Washington consistently either did not or lacked the moral courage to give it due weight in his actions as President. Indeed – even if he had statesmanlike reasons – Washington showed a lack of moral courage in 1793 – and betrayed his implied own moral principles! [He had reasons (e.g. to keep the Union intact) but they should not excuse the terrible evil he continued – in signing The Fugitive Slave Act.]

It was only very, very gradually – and after very much further thought on the causes of the US Civil War that I came to realise that I did not agree with Lincoln's view of what Article IV of the (1788 and 1791) Constitutions said, Lincoln (and every other well-known US lawyer – except Alvan Stewart, some other abolitionists, and perhaps on occasion William Seward), believed that it mandated return of 'fugitive slaves' to their 'owners'. I hold that this Article can concern 'servants' and 'laborers' and 'not slaves: – I take the Article literally. But throughout American history to 1865 it was generally held as 'The Fugitive Slave Clause'.

This is what we shall meet again and again in this book! This is what, for historical reasons, must be called [– 'The Fugitive Slave Clause'. However it does not mention 'slaves'! Nor, I argue, does it refer to slaves! [Even though from 1788 to 1865 (at least) it was almost always believed to refer to slaves]. Congressmen, State legislatures, lawyers and Judges all believed it referred to slaves. But in Chapter 2 I shall prove it does not. First, however, the clause must be stated in full – so I turn now to Authorities.

AUTHORITIES

First I cite below in (my) Section 1, from the 1788 US Constitution – Article IV, Section 2, paragraph 3 – which was read as giving Federal Authority to 'deliver-up' 'escaped' slaves to someone claiming them. Then I give many reasons why the paragraph was so read. Then I show that this reading was a misconceived one. Yet, (for instance because the 1791 US Constitution contains the same Article IV, paragraph 3, which by 1791 was very generally held to be about fugitive slaves), for historical reasons this paragraph was called 'The Fugitive Slave Clause'. This is ironic – since my chapters will show that fugitive slaves were not the people denoted or described in paragraph 3 of Article IV. No doubt they were intended as the denotation(s).

I begin (all) this work in Section 2 which follows. Notice the 1791 Constitution was the US Supreme Law. (The 1791 US (Amended) Constitution remains the 'Supreme Law' of the USA). The 1791 Constitution is to be read with great carefulness.

For the misconception I correct had grave consequences – great violence both to many slaves and (some) free people resulted from a sheer misconception on what the Constitution(s) said. It can be validly called 'Customary Law' – was it Constitutional (Law)?? (It was in the US Constitution(s) – but it never stated what people believed it did.) In Section 4 here I give individual great authorities on the history, law and concepts involved.

I myself am not a lawyer nor an historian. I am a philosopher who aims to attend closely to (what I think to be) the logical structure and logical implications of the whole 1791 Constitution. Because of these interests and because I hold the 1791 Constitution (now as amended – but up to [early] 1865 as unamended), is and was a living document which Americans (and others) could understand, I do not always cleave closely to the special legal rules which lawyers – in 1788 or 1791 – or even 1820 – used in reading it!!

Section 1

So please notice carefully that – for instance as it is ambiguous – I give a novel reading of 'The Fugitive Slave Clause'. But

    (a) I do not deny that this paragraph was taken by most Americans, (e.g. almost all US lawyers, Judges and (other) State and Federal officials), as being about fugitive slaves. So, for historical reasons, I call it – 'The Fugitive Slave Clause' – (it would be pedantic to always refer to it as paragraph 3 of Section 2, Article IV).

    (b) I do not deny that this misunderstanding, [which was held by Federal Courts (not just State ones)], in fact ruled the way (most) 'fugitive slaves' were (violently) treated ('delivered up' to 'the party' who 'claimed' them): that is why I allow it was 'Customary Law';

    (c) But I affirm that the paragraph did not mention, specify or refer to slaves (even 'fugitive slaves')!

I shall argue this conceptual point in the relevant way – i.e. through points of definition, conceptual structure and logical inference.

The precise wording of paragraph 3 of Section 2 of Article IV (of the 1788 and 1791 US Constitution) is:

> *'No person held to service or labor in one State, under the laws thereof, escaping into another, shall, in consequence of any law or regulation therein, be discharged from such service or labor but shall be delivered up on Claim of the party to whom such service or labor may be due.'*
> (My italics)

Even one reading of this paragraph reveals that it:

    (a) Does not specify 'slaves' literally (or 'owners'); and

    (b) It assumes certain persons have 'escaped'; and

    (c) The claimant may be a stranger! Indeed the claimant might be a chancer, a crook, even a criminal just out of jail.

Yet this paragraph was (generally) believed to mean that (all) slaves who left their 'owner's' State (except in the presence of the 'owner');

(A) had 'escaped' (illegally); and
(B) were fugitives; and
(C) were still owned by some 'party' (for instance, who had bought them but not necessarily – they might be 'delivered' to someone else!); and
(D) could be 'claimed' by 'a party', (as we saw not necessarily the 'owner' – or, even, law-abiding!); and
(E) were then to be 'delivered up', back to 'the party' (who claimed ownership!), usually by force. The claim might be false! Free 'blacks' could be – and were – 'delivered' into slavery! It is true the 'party' (or his agent) might go before a Magistrate – but this did not ensure true claims.

The paragraph meant none of this! Not a single one of these points survives a study of what logically the paragraph means or implies! This is a very surprising conclusion. Let us see how it is reached.

Section 2

Even a casual (second) reading of paragraph 3 shows decisively:

(a) it is about persons;
(b) who give service or labor, as they are 'held to this. The word is not – 'forced' to labor, nor 'bound to labor'! Hence it must be presumed that the servants and laborers are free people – since the Constitution itself (in Article I) uses the much stronger terms, 'bound to service . . .' of free people!! (This is a major point – unnoticed by most scholars – so I repeat the Constitution does not say this 'service' or 'labor' is 'bound');
(c) under a US State's laws;
(d) but are assumed to have 'escaped';
(e) and who might be 'claimed' by some 'party' (unknown to them whose 'claim' rests on assertion only in the first instance). Notice that a 'party' in a given State might claim a

'negro' in another as his slave! For he could say "This man is an escaped slave".

(f) the 'claim' is not required to be made by anyone who has even seen the servant or labourer! (Or made to a Court). And the Claimant – even if a liar! – can activate agents to use force to bring him a (free) 'negro'. (No-one who did not read the clause itself would believe such points – they are incredible. But they are within the scope of the clause.)

These points at once undermine the idea that the 'party' is necessarily claiming his (or her) 'property'. They also show a fugitive (slave) may have 'moved'. 'Escaped' is a prejudicial judgement.

Notice:

(1) a 'fugitive' slave is (by the structure of Article IV) not a fugitive from justice! (Since paragraph 2 deals with them!) Indeed, paragraph 3 deals with no crime of 'escape'! (Paragraph 2 only deals with crimes.) In fact paragraph 3 deals with no crime of the slave – rather it is the claimant who may be and have been guilty of crimes!! (State laws may impute crime to the slave – but that is exactly what the Federal Constitution avoids doing – or even saying the person is 'a slave');

(2) the slave has fled;

(3) has fled justly (not 'escaped'!);

(4) the clause is so written that it encourages false 'claims' and abusive behaviour (directly contrary to the peace of the United States) by such a wide class of claimants that some may, (as we saw) be criminals and could in theory be fugitives from justice themselves! But it was in the Federal Constitution(s). This however is not the main point – since it is contradicted by other Articles!

(5) the clause does not put in place any Federal (legal) checking mechanisms on claims;

(6) it allows, under cover of some 'claim' someone believes – or says he believes! – valid, both kidnap (e.g. of free 'blacks') and violence (to 'slaves'). Incidentally it also 'allows' violence to free blacks (kidnapped by 'slave hunters')! (Some slaves were later emancipated – most were in forced labor for life!)

(7) does not distinguish 'labor' with the forced labor for life imposed on (most) US slaves,

(8) confuses forced work with service. True service (like true labor), is inherently under the control of the worker – (in this case the servant);

(9) tacitly allows violence to the slave or other person claimed – contrary to at least three aims of the US Constitution(s), Justice, Liberty and 'Domestic Tranquillity'. The violence is tacitly allowed as the 'slave' must be 'delivered up'.

To say a slave has escaped is to assume his or her slavery is:

(10) lawful – in Federal Law (which overrides State law if necessary);

(11) not grossly unjust.

I deny both (1) and (2). Slavery was not, (I argue), decisively proved lawful under Federal Law. And it was grossly unjust! Supreme Court Decisions are not to the point – the two relevant ones *Barron v. Baltimore* and *Dred Scott v. Sandford* show ignorance of what a Federal Constitution was. In particular, they do not even see that 'the Supreme Law' must override State laws (if they conflict).

Section 3

But could The Fugitive Slave Clause be a <u>technical</u> term whose only meaning was:

> "No person enslaved in one State (by State law there) may escape into another State but must be delivered up . . ."

No, it could not as –

(1) This at once raises the issue that persons who are said in an earlier part of the Constitution to be "bound to service' would be (for that time) in a closer enslavement. For if 'held to labor . . . ..' were a technical term so would be 'bound to service'!

(2) A second issue would be – how was it discovered these were (someone holds) technical terms? Constitutional Interpretation

would then be thrown into confusion. For instance is the 'General Welfare of the US' a technical term meaning only 'Peace in the USA'. No – looking for technical terms is fruitless.

(3) And even had the Clause been a technical term does it concern both life-long Slaves and also those now enslaved but later emancipated? How is that found out?

(4) And when – earlier – 'Relations between the States', (e.g. States recognising laws of and in others) is a topic is that a technical term? Does it mean only relations between State legislatures – so that citizens outside the legislatures are not involved?

No – it isn't a technical term. And generally the search for technical terms is a dead end.

(5) Finally and conclusively even if it was a technical term (which it is not), slaves as such still come under some provisions of The Bill of Rights – as they are permanently called persons.

The conceptual structure of the 1791 US Constitution gives all persons in the US some rights, ('Indians' were persons!). Further even when persons in the US travel they do not thereby lose rights – though if they change nationality they may notice –

(A) The grant of legislative powers by the US people does not extend to open-ended, abusive law. (If it did even citizens would not be safe.)

(B) No Constitutional definition is given even of 'unfree person' – let alone of 'slave'! Nor is any such definition given of 'free person'. In particular' permanent, captive slavery is never mentioned or specified in the 'Supreme Law'.

The reasoning for (A) is simple. If the US Supreme Law could contain law relating to any 'party' who may 'claim' any slave who has crossed State lines and decree enslavement or re-enslavement of a 'fugitive slave' then it could also decree that, for instance, any naturalised citizen be suspended from US citizenship on 'claim' of any 'party' who 'testifies' to a Magistrate the person was a criminal. The latter is Unconstitutional – so then is the former. Therefore it cannot be Constitutional Law – however many Supreme Court judgments uphold it!

The reasoning on (B) is this:

Under the (so-called) 'Fugitive Slave Clause' any party can put in a 'claim' – unverified and sometimes unverifiable – to have 'delivered up' to him (i.e. the party), a person who may be free (This happened.)

Logically it is a sound argument, (in practice not allowed) for the 'slave' to deny that the 1788 and 1791 US Constitution has any word, 'slave', or any definition of 'slave' or even any definition of 'unfree' person! The slave could truly claim he or she was in fact unfree – but not – by Federal definition – either enslaved or a slave! For instance, he had Article IV of The Bill of Rights: so he was not Constitutionally a slave.

If the reply to these points was – 'State laws make you a slave' he could say:

"You have no right to hold these are in accord with the Supreme Law of the USA, where in Article 1, Section 2, paragraph 3: 'The Apportionment Clause'; certain 'unfree persons' in the USA are explicitly to be counted, (in this case meaning – enumerated), for purposes of representation of the people! Hence no State has the right to make its de facto 'slave' laws determine either permanent loss of freedom or no Constitutional status for 'unfree persons'. Note that some 'unfree' persons must – (not may) – be counted for Representation of the People! So they must be available for counting. And they are needed for Representation of the People! This proves incidentally that it breaks Federal Law to violently detain even a slave – since he or she may be needed to count – and so to move to the count.

Section 4

If paragraph 3 of Article IV of the (1788 and 1791) US Constitution really was a 'Fugitive Slave Clause' it was:

(a) destructive of 'Justice, Liberty and Domestic Tranquillity', which the Constitution(s) explicitly say (in The Preamble) they aim to achieve for 'the people of the United States'.

Notice that even if – as the majority of scholars held and hold – these people are US citizens (only), the clause is still directly destructive of each aim (as – to take one of many examples – free 'blacks' and 'slaves' can be kidnapped – contrary to all three aims).

(b) also anti-democratic; (hence an insult to The Declaration of Independence (which rests just government on consent of the governed generally (not only 'State citizens' of US States).

But a critic will say:

'Since it was intended to be about certain slaves and was understood (generally) to be about them – what else could the clause possibly be about?'

I answer – exactly what the words say:

'Persons who are held to service or labor under a State's laws. That is – certain servants and laborers.' In particular – indentured laborers and State servants – e.g. those servants who work for State Courts.

The critic will say:

'These must be slaves!'

I answer: How can persons who serve or labor be necessarily slaves? [A slave is a captive, forced laboror under the (usual) life-long control and punishment of someone else!]

Why then did the 'clause' have such a hold on the American political consciousness as to be read – and misconceived – as 'The Fugitive Slave Clause'? Notice the deceptive pretence that slaves give service or labor. Then among the other reasons were:

(1) the intentions of the writers(s);
(2) the very wide existence of slavery in many US States;
(3) an unwillingness to probe the lives, conditions and sufferings of slaves;
(4) belief that 'the South' wanted slavery embedded in Southern States (as was true at many times);

(5) false beliefs that slavery was an unchangeable 'Institution';

(6) also false belief that the Union was inextricably bound up with US slavery for ever;

(7) an oversight that Article IV – which appeared to be about relations of US States! – contained – (paragraph 3) – a full scale attempt to lay down a law governing (so-called) 'escaped slaves' for all time! But they were not deemed 'slaves'. (That would have exposed the deceit in the clause.) There was licence to make (unchecked) claims and powers (concealed in the clause) to activate 'agents', (not necessarily lawyers), to lay hands on 'persons', sometimes citizens of other States, or emancipated slaves – or 'free blacks'!, and 'slaves' (who always had very little power, if any). And – in the case of any person 'claimed' – to 'deliver them' 'back' by violence. If this does concern relations of US States it directly causes their conflict! It tends directly to cause conflict with 'Free States'. Indeed it was one cause of the US Civil War. (It was also a potential cause of violence in a few 'Territories');

(8) deference to what were thought of as Constitutional rules;

(9) finally, widespread and oppressive knowledge that some slave-owners would use sheer power to get their way come what may – often masking the force by emphasising 'States' rights' and sometimes US Supreme Court judgments (e.g. the really fatuous judgment of the Supreme Court of 1835 – that The Bill of Rights did not hold against the States – which showed that the Justices even failed to understand exactly what the US Constitution of 1791 was!)! This judgment was *Barron v. Baltimore*.

There were various other reasons which historians may investigate or have made plain. But these nine reasons go some way to explain popular readings of paragraph 3 as a 'Fugitive Slave Clause'. And lawyers also were deceived (and advised clients the clause was essentially about escaped slaves).

Section 5

Lawyers should have exposed the abusive open-ended nature of Article IV in Section 2, paragraph 3 in 1788. Paragraph 3 should never have been let pass as a possible element in a (Federal) Constitution. For it allowed – more exactly it presumed any Tom, Dick or Harry could 'claim' whatever 'black' person in another State he thought he could get away with as a slave. Perhaps some lawyers (Abolitionists are candidates) did expose it rigorously between 1788 and 1791? But this is not yet a matter of record so far as I know.

But most lawyers were thoroughly duped by it. So were very, very many ordinary Americans. In the popular US consciousness after 1788 there was a (very) active belief that it was 'The Fugitive Slave Clause'. It caused untold evil, cruelty and conflict between 'Slave' States and 'Free' States. The Fugitive Slave Acts of 1793 and 1850 drove the conflict even further.

The clause was skilfully concealed in Article IV to make it appear as if it was de jure a right (to claim fugitive 'slaves'). I deny that any US lawyers (even the Supreme Court) ever had authority ample enough to identify US State 'slave' status with a status of life-long enforced captivity under ('recognised in') Federal Law. But it cannot be denied that US (States) slaves were (usually) life-long forced captives both of 'a party' and in and of a State. Hence it really was unconstitutional to sanction life-long US slavery.

Since even such slaves could – in theory – be emancipated, was it a valid inference to say that in Federal Law 'slaves' as such were permanently 'unfree'? I doubt it. So no 'party' who claimed a fugitive slave was, I argue, accurate in Federal Law – at most he could claim an 'unfree' laborer! Even then he would – I argue – have to prove to Federal officials the person was unfree in the State he had fled to (which was often false).

I don't deny – how could I? – that the US Supreme Court held (after 1803 in *Marbury V. Madison),* it had authority to interpret the (1791) US Constitution and in a sense held that some US States, had 'laws' on 'slaves', and that they used the description, 'slave', of certain persons. What I deny is that the last point was part of a reading consistent with either the US 'Supreme Law' (the 1791 Constitution), or what Lincoln called the 'Organic Law (of the US) – which, he held, preceded the Constitution(s).

AUTHORITIES

It is time to turn to authorities on such issues.

But first there is an important fact – little recognised at the time – that the 1788 US Constitution alone gave Congress powers sufficient to be used to abolish US slavery! For instance, Congress had those powers 'necessary to achieve' the general welfare of the United States – even if a certain power was not listed in the (1788) Constitution. (This point may have been denied by the Framers or the Congress). Much depends on what constituted 'the general welfare' of the people of the USA. But if it included (for instance), an end to cruelty to very many US residents, cruelty on a huge scale which was the case before, at, and after 1788, then Congress could – constitutionally – have ended US slavery – more exactly could have used its powers to that aim – since some US States would have resisted or left the Union! The 1791 US Constitution included The Bill of Rights. The great Abolitionist lawyer, Alvan Stewart, correctly saw – (by 1837) – that Article V of The Bill alone made existing US slavery illegal. Even the greatest lawyers in Lincoln's (Civil War) Cabinet – Lincoln himself, William Seward and Salmon Chase – had not seen this point so early. But Seward and Chase almost did so – and both fought many important legal battles (e.g. Chase in the *Matilda* case) against slave law(s)! Seward was also correct to speak of a 'Higher Law' – both Natural Law and the 'OrganicLaw'.

Lincoln always thought slavery evil. Also he believed there was an 'Organic Law'. Lincoln reverenced both US Constitutions too much to see through 'The Fugitive Slave Clause' to the sham it was. Though he was always a moral critic of the evil of (US and other) slavery. He would – of course – have been right to claim the clause was in the text of the 1791 Constitution. And also right to think Washington, among others, had no objection to it at the time.

However advances in logic in the last two hundred years now allow a very acute analysis of the language in Article IV – and then in The Bill of Rights – which explodes for ever the pretence that concepts such as 'chattel slave' were mentioned anywhere in (the 1788 or 1791) US Constitutions. Logicians distinguish – at the level of language – descriptions from predication(s), – at the level of sense – defined concepts and inherently vague ones – at the level of objects – individual objects and classes. Chattel slave is a concept necessarily involving captivity and enforced 'possession' (of someone) and

xxv

forced-work. Only certain descriptions or predications have that sense. None are in Article IV, Section 2, paragraph 3! (i.e. if my arguments are valid).

The concept of '(US) chattel slave' is not referred to in either the 1788 or 1791 Constitution – at most (certain) 'unfree' persons are. And since they can be – and sometimes were later 'free persons' (due to emancipation) even the Constitutional texts – including 'The Fugitive Slave Clause' – could not and did not denominate them slaves, [who (as we have seen), are – and were in the US – generally life-long captives of 'owners' (and in fact also of States].

It will be said that State 'slave' laws were so rigid they implied slavery. This could be a hypothesis only. State 'Slave' Laws were changeable. So they did not necessarily, logically, imply life-long slavery, but they generally effected life-long, captive slavery of some people nevertheless.

Section 6

Here are the main works of scholarship which I have found most relevant to my study and which, so far as I know and can tell, reference every single historical point or event in it (save points on history in antiquity). (The conceptual and logical arguments and points being mine alone.)

Jacobus Ten Broek: *Equal Under Law* (Collier Books, New York, 1965) (This book is especially important for its accounts of the reasoning of great Abolitionist lawyers on the implications of the 1791 Bill of Rights.)

Seymour Drechsler: *Abolition: A History of Slavery and Anti-Slavery* (Cambridge University Press, 2010)

Gordon Wood: *The American Revolution* (Weidenfeld and Nicolson, 2002)

Robert Harvey: *A Few Bloody Noses* (John Murray, London 2001) Clinton Rossiter: *The First American Revolution* (Harcourt Brace, New York, 1956)

Jeremy Black:	*George III* (Yale University Press, 2006)
Colin Bonwick:	*The American Revolution* (Palgrave Macmillan, 2005) (see pages 36–74, 181–199 – but others are many)
William Hague:	*Wilberforce* (Harper Press, 2009)
Robert M Ketchum:	*The World of George Washington* (American Heritage Company, 1974)
Esmond Wright:	*Washington and the American Revolution* (Pelican, Penguin, 1975)
John Stuart Mill:	*On Liberty* (ed. G. Himmelfarb) (Penguin Books, 1974)
Robert Natelson:	*The Original Constitution* (Tenth Amendment [Notice Professor Natelson holds that the FSC was (1788-1862 or 1865) Constitutional Law. (I dissent).
William Lloyd	*(A Sermon) The Dangers of the Nation* (Boston, Garrison 1829) (see also under J. A. Scott (II))
Frederick Law	*The Cotton Kingdom* (1861, then 1953 – A.A. Olmsted: Knopf, New York)
Leonard Bacon:	*Slavery: Essays 1833–1846* (Mnesnosyne Co., Miami, Florida, 1969)
John Anthony Scott (I):	*Hard Trials on My Way* (Mentor Books, New American Library, 1974) (especially chapters 5–12 and the Bibliography, pp. 277–286)
John Anthony Scott (II):	*Living Documents in America* (ed.) (New York, Washington Square Press, 1964)
Horace Mann:	*Slavery: Letters and Speeches* (Mnesnosyne (Publishing) Co., Miami, Florida, 1969)
Laurence M. Friedman:	*A History of American Law* (Simon and Schuster, New York, 1975)
Keith Hamilton & Patrick Salmon:	*Slavery, Diplomacy and Empire* (eds.) Sussex Academic Press, 2010)
Henry David Thoreau:	*Walden and Civil Disobedience* (Longman, 2002. Introduction by Michael Messer) (Stanley Cavell has argued that Thoreau intended Walden not only as a criticism of

the United States of the time (its materialism) but as a (sort of) scripture. Cavell may be right. However if he is, it is a tragedy that Thoreau included in the book an ill-thought out aside on US ('Negro") slavery which appears to ignore its great evil – or make it appear less than it was. *Civil Disobedience* is far more forthright in its condemnation of US slavery. It is a landmark in strategy against unjust State power – and it influenced Gandhi and Martin Luther King.)

Kenneth Stampp: *The Peculiar Institution* (Eyre and Spotiswoode, London, 1964)
[This is a measured and thorough indictment of US slavery in the South, taking into account its rather sporadic growth – and the fact that many Southerners (e.g. many slave-owners), never foresaw its gravest consequences! But its wealth of detailed reference brings out the sheer cruelty of the practice for 'blacks' at each stage. As with the other major US historians of slavery, Stampp calls it an 'Institution': I call it a 'practice', and give conceptual arguments in my book for this major change of classification.]

Louie J. Archer: *Slavery and Other Forms of Unfree Labor* (ed.) (Routledge, London and New York, 1988) (Especially notable for new perspectives on US slavery are the Essays I, II, 12, 13, and 18. So for slavery worldwide are pages 280–297.)

Booker, T. Washington *Up From Slavery* (Lancer Books, New York, 1968)
[This author, an educationalist, who had escaped slavery is notably kind and generous in his discussion of some Southern slave-holders. He also sees slavery as an

Institution (which I deny – seeing it as a practice) and some Southerners as 'victims'! (as well as the slaves!) I would say (rather) that (e.g. Southern), slave-holders were compliant rather than victims. (Many were (as far as I understand the evidence – in Kenneth Stampp's book), cruel not only compliant). But Booker T. Washington – like Frederick Douglass and Henry Highland Garnett, who were also escaped slaves – was a character of great compassion and vision and knew more about slavery than I do!]

Alexander Smellie:	*The Journal of John Woolman* (Andrew Melrose, 1898)
Joel Schor:	*Henry Highland Garnett* (Greenwood Press, 1977)
Frederick Douglass:	*My Bondage and My Freedom* (first published New York 1850, now Dover Books) see also *Narrative of the Life of an American Slave* (Belknap Press, 1960)
Benjamin Quarles:	*Black Abolitionists* (New York, Oxford University Press, 1969)
Doris Kearns Goodwin:	*Team of Rivals* (Penguin Books, Great Britain, 2009)
Helen Hill Miller:	*The Case for Liberty* (North Carolina University Press, 1965, see pages 212–218 in particular)
Hugh Brogan:	*The Longman History of the United States* (Longman, 1999)
Chris Cook & David Waller:	*The Longman Handbook of United States History*
James Randall:	*Lincoln the President* (Illinois University Press, Eyre & Spottiswoode, 1953)
James Randall:	*Lincoln and the South* (Illinois University Press)
James Randall:	*The Civil War and Reconstruction* (Illinois University Press; Little, Brown & Company, January 1937)

J. F. Maxwell:	*Slavery and the Catholic Church* (Barry Rose Publishers, 1975)
David Reynolds:	*America: Empire of Liberty* [Allen Lane (Penguin, 2009)]
Gary Nash:	*The Unknown American Revolution* (Jonathan Cape, 2000)
Kenneth C. Wheare:	*Abraham Lincoln and the United States* (Hodder and Stoughton, 1948) (This book is an excellent and judicious summary of Lincoln's career. There were more than 10,000 volumes on aspects of Lincoln's life as of 1948 – and since then there may be very many more. I give two on his life only – there may be 200 more! – and one on his Civil War trials – again at least 200 may now have come out.)
George McGovern:	*Abraham Lincoln* (Thorndike Press, May 2009)
H. G. Pitt:	*Abraham Lincoln* (Sutton Publishing Limited, Illustrated Edition, March 1998)
Eric Foner:	*The Fiery Trial* (Wiley, UK, 2011) [For the period after Lincoln's assassination – the Presidency of Andrew Johnson with the inception of 'Reconstruction; and also of new 'Black Codes' in the (US) South – see also my own book: –
Norman Coles:	*Interpreting Political Events in the USA* (Sussex Academic Press, 2009, Chapter 2 in particular)]
E de la Boetie:	*Discourse on Disobedience*
Louis Dumont:	*Homo Hierarchicus* (both the last two books – very rare – might be available in part via Wikipedia)
Alex Hayley:	*Roots* (Hutchinson) [This book falls into two contrasting parts. The first, which studies life in Africa of Kunta Kinte, an ancestor of Alex Hayley, shows the life was communitarian, peaceful

and respected ecology. The second, beginning with Chapter 33, details the appalling, horrific, sadistic cruelty and neglect – done by those who captured, then those who shipped the slaves and by those who ran the slaves' work (e.g. 'owners' and overseers) in America. The cruelty in all phases was so extreme I was unable even to read more than a few pages of it! It must be among the worst set of crimes ever recorded!]

James Walrin: *The Zong* (Harvard University Press, 2011) [On this ship slaves were murdered by being brutally thrown overboard – women as well as men, young as well as mature. The great Abolitionist, Granville Sharp, researched and proved this and took to Court a (former) Governor!]

I would also like to bring to attention William Miller's excellent *A New History of the United States* (Andesite Press; original publication 1970; available in scanned format via Amazon). Miller's work is particularly good on the 1775–1865 period.

Chapter 1

All slavery was and is inhuman. Chattel slavery, where a human person is owned and has (in practice) no human or legal rights, is wicked and evil. Yet in many societies chattel slavery has been a common practice and entrenched by law. [Even in Israel at various times slavery existed – for instance, King Solomon used the work of slaves (and others), for building projects. Whether this was chattel slavery I do not know – but even if not it was unhuman for the slaves. In some Greek city States there were many slaves. Athens was one. Sparta treated 'helots' as (harshly controlled) slaves – even if they were not so called].

Rome regularly enslaved hundreds of thousands of conquered people (the total figure might be millions) and took slaves to Rome. (These figures are ones I estimate to be likely – given the great scale of Roman war, conquest and practice to enemy 'States'. But I am not an historian of Rome. And these figures might be too high. Scholars may correct them – and as I say they are estimates). Unfortunately so potent and widespread was this enslavement leading to a (forced) Roman order, (both in 'provinces' and Rome), that even St Peter (in his first Epistle) and St Paul, were quite accustomed to it as a type of social structure – and (both) enjoined obedience for slaves!

Thankfully St James took an extreme anti-slavery view – condemning any discrimination in treatment of people based on any kind of class or status. St James went as far as condemning ever thinking of discrimination (of all kinds), against the poor. (Slaves particularly would have been emancipated had his teaching been followed.)

In context however St Peter's and St Paul's advice to slaves:

(a) may reflect that they knew that in fact slaves (of the Romans)

1

were vulnerable (having no legal status in a Court for instance) and if advised to rebel might be killed;

(b) allows that slaves (and Christians) might be persecuted if advised to discountenance slavery; also brutally killed;

(c) both Apostles tried to get humane treatment for slaves;

(d) both also saw and championed (by their theologies) the humanity of slaves.

Authorities on that period tell us that these two Apostles would have effected more evils (particularly for slaves) had they openly championed freedom (for slaves). While this must be born in mind I personally think that their advice (to slaves) went beyond 'obedience' – and was 'total submission'. I think this may not take into full account slave-owners' cruel practice. (But slaves were 'emancipated' on occasions). I personally think St Peter and St Paul could have (alternatively), either not written at all on slavery or said that some Roman lawyers thought slavery 'against the law of nature' or, like St James, have said any class distinction was wrong.

St James' teaching seems to me the best option – a real option then. Yet more than seventeen hundred years after St James wrote we find many British people not only colluding in the enslavement of Africans (by buying them from traders), but transporting them in especially terrible conditions on slave-ships to the West Indies or to North America – for sale and further slavery. (British sponsored and trans-ported) slavery was endemic in the colonial West Indies. It was very widespread in the British 'colonies' in North America. (For instance, it was greatly encouraged by British Authorities in regard to New Jersey – regarded as a 'beneficial' (God help us!) and usual practice). Nor did (British) Governors in other colonies (in the eighteenth century) move for its Abolition – not even I believe going so far as to take up the issue with colonial assemblies! So – contrary to what might seem the case – the British record in regard to slavery (before the nineteenth century) was probably far worse than the American record – though that was (also) extremely cruel. It was in the British American colonies that a slave was burned – (see the Editor's Introduction to *The Journal of John Woolman*. (The practice however lasted into the days of the Union: Hugh Brogan tells us that a slave was burned in 1806.)

Slavery in the colonial West Indies was vocally defended by many MPs. As we saw the British Governments or the Governors of colonies or the Colonial Assemblies themselves never moved to abolish it in America.

Chapter 2

We must not confuse slavery with a slave trade – though the latter does perpetuate the former. And both are evil. Slavery is enforced and unjust captivity of an individual human person by an 'owner' (or group of them – or agents), who claims the person as property and at whose will and disposal the person must act (unless sold or died) and work. We saw that in the Roman Empire some (not many) slaves were freed before death. In the USA most slaves had to work for an 'owner till death'!

Notice that the slave, although (almost always) made a 'forced laborer', is not technically or necessarily a labourer (who can decide to labor or not). The slave may be forced, for example to train animals, to do housework, or to keep accounts. In fact, Doris Kearns Goodwin – rightly – distinguishes slaves from laborers (in Washington for example).

Still less is the slave a servant – nor does he or she give service, which is voluntary and free! In sum and in strict definitions a slave cannot be either a laborer or a servant! (This is true even when slaves are given high positions by, for instance, a tyrant.) 'Military Service' is very often compulsory – so is not service in the first sense. 'Domestic Service' given to (or forced on) slaves is also not service in the first sense.

It follows logically that one 'held to service or labor under the laws thereof' cannot when so defined be a slave! People may resist my conclusion because they believe the words 'held to . . . ' and ' . . . under the laws thereof' mean that 'the laws' have some binding force which converts forced labor into either 'service' or 'labor'. But that is – when so stated – a conceptual mistake! Forced labor is not and cannot be either 'service' or 'labor' even if someone is held to it (or other directives of an 'owner'), by State law(s). Forced labor, like slavery itself, allows no scope for an individual to serve (give

4

'service'), or work when he chooses as a laborer. However, US Constitutional experts in the period from 1788 to 1863 did hold the clause to be about slaves! Most eminent scholars (e.g. Hugh Brogan) now do so.

I argue that the clause, though intended to apply to fugitive slaves – and almost invariably believed to refer to slaves – and also enforced on fugitive slaves – and finally, textually and literally in the 1788 and 1791 Constitutions, and so in a sense 'Constitutional' never referred to slaves! I grant of course that it was almost invariably taken – except by some Quakers and Abolitionists – to give authority to recapture fugitive slaves.

I also grant that so many Americans took the paragraph as 'referring' to slaves that in practice it is not inaccurate to say that people 'referred' to slaves with it. But the paragraph neither mentioned, meant or had reference to slaves of any kind – even fugitive slaves! (The reader should be warned that Lincoln, who was a great lawyer as well as a great politician, statesman and President, is more likely to be right on Article IV than I am!) I recognise of course:

(a) that it concerns 'service' and 'labor' under the laws of a State; and

(b) this makes a case for holding that some such 'labor' (e.g. in Southern States) was not labor but slavery; and

(c) that both the Constitutional Framers and a great majority of US citizens took it as about slaves.

But I deny that slavery is 'labor' under the State's laws! It is captivity – whereas 'labor' is under a laborer's control and initiation. Indeed, good US historians sharply distinguish laborers from slaves! So did poor laborers! These facts speak for themselves – and in favour of my interpretation.

But my reading of Article IV is unorthodox . . . In this book I defend it in great detail . . . I also aim to show that it logically implies that the (so called) 'Fugitive Slave Clause' was – from 1791 – wholly unconstitutional! It was inconsistent with other Articles (Article I of the Constitution – also with Articles I, IV and V of The Bill of Rights).

Of course, it is part of the written text of both Constitutions. But this is cancelled by the fact that numerous other statements of the 1791 Constitution directly contradict it if it is interpreted as about fugitive slaves! For instance by Article I (The Apportionment Clause) a certain number of 'unfree' persons must be counted – yet among these may well be slaves hidden by agents who come to 'deliver them up'. So the Fugitive Slave Clause is not consistent with The Apportionment Clause yet the latter clause is essential to Representation of the US people in Congress.

Yet fugitive slaves were violently reclaimed because of a supposed authority (of the Fugitive Slave Clause).

Chapter 3

I use against the usual reading (of Article IV) – paragraph 3) five major kinds of argument:

(1) textual;
(2) definitional;
(3) conceptual (often about the implications of defined or undefined concepts, and the relationships between concepts);
(4) historical;
(5) legal.

From my arguments some interesting consequences follow about the relation of slavery in the States to the Constitutions and the Union.

I grant that both Constitutions recognise State laws, (for instance, one State is not allowed to invade and overturn the laws of another). But I deny that State laws are necessarily in accord with Constitutional law! I think it doubtful whether any State laws regarding slavery (even when clothed in misleading language which masked their purpose), were allowed by the whole 1791 Constitution. I think this view can be supported by an enumeration of the rights in The Bill of Rights! So I argue that all 'slaves' after 1791 were 'captives' (of their 'owners' and of some States). I realise this is a view of few scholars. But if my arguments are valid it follows that deference to the practice of 'slavery' even in nearly all American Federal Law Courts from 1791 to 1860 was misconceived . . . (I grant, however, that if The Bill of Rights only ever mentioned rights of US citizens then it is harder to sustain my reasoning. But I deny that Article 5 of the Bill of Rights is only about US citizens).

The practice of State Law Courts in making decisions on slaves was, on my arguments, unconstitutional unless they, in each case, allowed appeals to Federal Courts. And even Federal Courts misread Article IV (Section 2, paragraph 3). The paragraph is about people who labor or serve – not slaves! Notice very carefully they are not described as 'unfree persons'!

Chapter 4

Notice carefully that

(1) the US Constitutions of 1788 – and more importantly and notably – of 1791 were intended to have a living authority which could be found (and applied e.g. in Federal Courts) by future US citizens (e.g. of 1810, 1820, 1830, 1840 and so on);

(2) The posterity of US citizens were to have the benefit of e.g. the 1791 Constitution. Now taken in its normal sense this 'posterity' included children born where one parent was a 'slave' but the other a US citizen. (A point which can be denied – but which is worth much consideration at least.). And they were to enjoy Justice, Peace, Welfare and Liberty!

(3) It does not seem likely that even in 1791 some of the protections for US citizens in the Constitution (e.g. the protection in the Bill of Rights, Article IV against unreasonable seizures) would not have been given to those eminent soldiers – for instance Baron de Kalb – who had fought for US Independence. Yet they were foreigners – not US citizens.

Since the 1791 Constitution (including The Bill of Right as an essential part of the 1791 Constitution) was to have a living authority and one that could be consulted by Federal Courts and one that was expressed in public words which had meanings [and these determined mainly by (previous) regular use of those words in a community – e.g. that of English-speaking Americans – but also of for instance English writers like Johnson – and also English lawyers (like Lord Mansfield), even, American lawyers were not completely free to appeal to wholly new meanings which bore little relation to their use in those communities which gave rise to them.]

It was also true – as Constitutional scholars (Professor Robert

Natelson in his writings), point out that the 1791 US Constitution arose in a legal context and both the original aims of the framers and the understanding of legal terms were and are important for understanding it.

But this point does not change or override the point that the 1791 Constitution had to be understood – and one essential part of understanding it was the public use of words (e.g. the word 'person').

It logically follows that:

(A) ironically if the 'Fugitive Slave Clause' considered in 1791 were about 'slaves' then since it explicitly states 'No person held to service or labor . . . ' The Bill of Rights must give rights to slaves!.. The Bill explicitly states that no person may be deprived of various rights! To liberty for instance!.. Since, then persons may not be deprived of liberty (save criminals duly and legally tried by jury trial) it follows logically:

(B) that slaves may not be;

(C) and therefore The Fugitive Slave Clause is at once invalid and illegal – (since it violates Article V of The Bill of Rights!).

Chapter 5

It is not correct to jump to the conclusion that the 'persons' in paragraph 3 of Section 2 of Article IV, ('the Fugitive Slave Clause'), cannot be persons according to The Bill of Rights. If anything, since the Amended Constitution of 1791 is the Supreme Law of the USA, The Bill of Rights and its Article IV are both included in the Supreme Law, so persons held to labor or service under a State's laws are – by specification and definition – persons (Constitutionally) and so persons to whom The Bill of Rights applies!

It is also invalid to argue to the conclusion that though slaves were (by the usual reading of both Articles I and IV persons, they failed to be persons as described in The Bill of Rights as Federal Courts did not 'free' slaves (till 1865). For The Bill of Rights constitutionally referred to them as persons! (Note that 'unfree' persons are persons.) There can be no possible doubt that 'slaves' were always persons – and constitutionally so.

It will be said – rightly – that the Supreme Court – for instance under Chief Justice Taney – held that slaves were not part of 'We the people of the USA' . . . This does not show that all particular mention of 'persons' in the 1791 Constitution cannot extend to slaves. Slaves could be persons in The Bill of Rights. This sounds contrary to fact and law! Since the Supreme Court was the lawful interpreter of what the Constitution (of 1791) stated and meant, it must be right when it judged such issues . . . But no – not necessarily!

For it was an undeniable fact that persons were referred to in Articles I and IV of the Constitution and these preceded the Bill of Rights both in the text and in time (i.e. from 1788). The Bill of Rights used exactly the same word, 'person', and even, as least once, the same phraseology, 'No person(s) . . . ! Hence logically – as meaning is mainly determined by public use of words – not even the Supreme Court could conclude that separate senses of the word 'person', were used at all in the 1791 Constitution. And had they been the Constitution would have been ambiguous.

Chapter 6

Moreover the wording of The Bill of Rights is specific and specifically chosen. It could have been quite different. It could have, for example, mentioned – 'State citizens' or 'citizens of the USA' or 'people of the USA'! It did not use any of these phrases – whether deliberately or unconsciously or by omission. It was specific in giving rights to persons – and was Constitutional. Also because it concerns rights (both of citizens and 'persons') every other clause of the US Constitution must conform to it! Must (– not may).

I do not ignore the fact that there were (some reasoned) Supreme Court judgments which denied the rights of US citizens to slaves and in effect limited The Bill of Rights to US citizens! Such judgments were to be expected! They expressed a very orthodox and reasonable view of the new 1791 Constitution – one that in the historical context may even be deemed the most reasonable one for any Judge to take.

But the point at issue here is whether there was a different rational view latent in the conceptual structure of the 1791 Constitution which also fitted better with its actual wording. There was – and it can be simply stated:

(1) a slave – as well as a 'free' man or woman – is (and was) a person;
(2) a person is an individual human being. Not the only kind of person (since God is three persons in one God) – but we are here concerned only with human persons in the USA);
(3) persons are given (some) rights in The Bill of Rights. More exactly individual human persons subject to US Federal Law are. So slaves are;
(4) Federal Law included 'the Fugitive Slave Clause' – but not as it was, usually, interpreted! (For the clause referred to servants and laborers.)

I grant that even by 1810 it was too soon for most lawyers to dispassionately examine what the exact wording of the 1791 Constitution logically implied. But that does not mean they were right to leave the issue aside!

From these considerations on 'person' and 'the people', as used in the 1791 Constitution it follows that a question at issue now is the conceptual meaning of the Preamble when the 1791 Constitution is read as one – and probably the main – enduring conceptual foundation for a lasting Federal Union. That question is not settled by noting that enslavement was an historical fact, or that Native Americans were unjustly treated in the nineteenth century. It needs a conceptual investigation. And given the work of such great scholars as Wood, Nash, Goodwin, James Macpherson, Hugh Brogan, Shelby Foote, Robert Harvey, Rob Natelson and Ronald Dworkin, this may be the time in which investigation of the question will bear much fruit.

I should also mention that I have consulted the tremendous book – *A History of American Law* by Lawrence Friedman (Simon and Schuster, New York, 1973) – and it confirms my views on the sheer evil, cruelty and inhumanity, not only of slavery but of State 'laws' on slavery. It does not however, concur with my view on the unconstitutionality of paragraph 3 of Article IV (of the 1788 and 1791 Constitution). This is my view and was implied by a few Abolitionist lawyers, even by 1840.

In case anyone supposes – wrongly – that I attribute all evils of enslavement and slavery in North America to Americans I should mention the overwhelming amount of evidence in *Wilberforce* (Harper Press, 2007), by William Hague that British traders and ships gave hundreds of thousands of enslaved people evil treatment in bringing them as slaves to America (e.g. in the 1730s, 1740s, 1750s and so on). Certainly many of the worst evils of slavery were perpetuated in American colonies and States. But not all.

There may be some reasons to read the phrase – 'We, the people of the United States . . . ' (from 1791) literally to mean the people (not just the citizens) of the US. But this is a view not held by most historians (or lawyers)! But no conceptual problem about how to read the Constitutions is solved by reading it as only US 'citizens'! In fact it then becomes even harder to hold that Article IV is Constitutional! For example, how can a sub-class of US residents in 1788 give

14

Congress all (necessary) powers to maintain 'the general welfare' and tranquillity, while:

(1) slaves are mistreated, flogged and violently 'delivered up' – and often sold away from their families and free 'blacks' may be 'delivered up' to slave-owners! (and all this in practice encouraged by The Fugitive Slave Clause).
(2) native Americans are treated as having few rights to their lands?
(3) 'Tories' (usually pro-British) though Americans – and citizens! – may be dispossessed and deported.

How can it be guaranteed by a sub-class of US residents that Congress has all necessary powers to maintain the general welfare?

Chapter 7

We can now look even more closely at the underlying conceptual and historical issues of whether the meaning of 'We, the people of the USA . . . ' was such that only citizens of the US States were deemed to be constitutionally such. The immediate historical answer (though not conceded to be so by 'free' blacks, some slaves and all Abolitionists – was), 'Yes, only citizens of the USA'.

Notice that this presupposes a clear account of 'citizen(s) of the USA'. As far as I know the only (plausible) one available in 1791 was – 'citizen of a State of the USA as a Federal Union of States'. Notice, now, that this leaves the definitions, in both cases (Federal and State), up to each State. There seems no immediate logical difficulty in this (though a codex would have to be given to say what each State defined as 'State citizen'). But there are practical difficulties:

(1) most Americans – not being lawyers – would not know in detail what the definition was (nor who were entitled to be 'citizens of the USA');

(2) the definition could change often – and at the will of any State (legislature) – i.e. the actual specifications of State citizens – and then 'citizens of the USA';

(3) if 'State citizens' were taken as 'free' then in turn 'free person of that State' would have to be explained – not just assumed;

(4) were 'State citizens' still 'free persons' when in prison?;

(5) slaves were unjustly 'unfree' (though no definitions of 'free' and 'unfree' were sometimes given by State legislatures!). But slaves were subject to State laws!! So they could argue they should be free – otherwise why were they unfairly and unjustly treated as under State laws? Did not some laws deprive them of liberty? (Contrary to The Bill of Rights.)

For all these reasons ((1) to (5) above) all Americans were – in 1791 – owed a conceptual account of why State citizenship should be the only (given, public, known), criterion of citizenship of the USA.

A simpler account of – 'We, the people of the USA' – would have been to say that this meant all those people (in the USA) resident and subject to State and Federal law. This might have had to be qualified slightly to exclude all visitors. But this made no difficulty – it could be phrased – 'all those persons in the USA who reside in the States and are always subject to Federal and State law'.

Historically the 'State citizen' account – (of 'US citizen') – held the field. So – since 'citizen of the US' was held to govern the sense of 'We, the people of the USA', and that in turn was (usually) held to determine which persons were given rights in The Bill of Rights, slaves and Native Americans were both excluded from those Constitutional rights. (This despite the fact both were persons and – on a clear basis of fact – among 'the people'.) Millions of US people held this usual account and Federal Courts held such a chain of reasoning. (But it was a theory which needed support.)

Could anything stand against this view which exposed its implications – (that 'the people of the USA' varied at the will and act of every individual State)? Not till, at the earliest, the 1840s.

But conceptually the view of some Abolitionists gave a reasoned account of 1791 Constitutional rights. This was that all people who lived in the USA were – as persons – entitled to (all) the rights in The Bill of Rights – given to persons! Thus slaves (and Native Americans) were so entitled. Note that these last classes – in contrast to quite a few citizens (such as Jefferson!) – were permanent residents of, [and (of course) in] the USA! (This fact might have been very important if only permanent residents of the USA were the class entitled to Constitutional rights.) Not all Abolitionists were sure that 'Indians' had Constitutional rights – but this reasoning applied to them as well as slaves. (Whether slaves were to have all rights given to 'the people' was a trickier issue, even for Abolitionists.)

The logical consequence of these conceptual points, taken together, was that the US Amended Constitution of 1791 was open to a new interpretation of both – 'We, the people of the USA' and 'person'. This was an interpretation that did not assume or presuppose that 'citizens of the USA' were the only persons mentioned in

The Bill of Rights. Logically this was to be expected – as the 1791 US Constitution was new – not a re-run of 1788 (though they overlapped!).

I grant the clear facts that, historically, neither John Adams nor Samuel Adams nor Patrick Henry, Madison nor Hamilton nor Washington aimed to make any such new interpretations! (Perhaps Jefferson or Franklin did at times? They had records which would have fitted with a new interpretation). But this does not rule out the reasonableness of a (new) conceptual interpretation.

We must always remember –

(a) the set of Constitutional statements in 1791 had to be consistent. If it was contradictory then the set was very likely to contain at least a false statement;
(b) The Bill of Rights had little point if it just affirmed that citizens were 'free' (since all agreed on that). Its (new) purpose was to give new legal rights to persons – and the conceptual issue was – who were as such persons?

It is an undeniable fact that most 'white' people in the USA, from 1788 to 1860, did not think slaves had Constitutional rights, nor did lawyers or Federal Courts. Supreme Court Justices also held such views and implied them in judgements. Historically this was not an unreasonable view at those times – though we must always remember that –
(
(a) Slaves had not been made such in the USA by 'due process of law'.
(b) Every enslaved person who came to the USA came having been unjustly (and very, very, often violently!), enslaved. To foreign observers it seemed very strange for a new Nation to sanction that by keeping them enslaved! Especially a nation which had officially stated all men were created free! If all men were created free thenUS slavery was unjust captivity.
(c) Some 'blacks' had been both free and citizens of a State.
(d) In 1772 Lord Chief Justice Mansfield had declared slavery repugnant to English law. This judgment had not been – even at that time – received in US law. But it could be argued that

it freed all slaves brought to America on, or by the agency of British ships before and from 1772 on. Also it could be argued that it was a precedent that should have been taken to apply in 1791 to all former 'British' slaves in North America − (i.e. in practice to American slaves). So (by, it must be admitted, a roundabout argument), 'American' slaves may be 'technically' free at the time of US Independence.

(e) Even US slavery did not exclude emancipation at some time so some (ex) slaves could be free men.

(f) The North-West Ordinance of 1787 had not permitted slavery to be extended to Ohio and the Great Lakes territories.

(g) 'Racial discrimination' was not a provision of the 1791 Constitution (unless 'Indian tribes', (so called) indicates this).

For all these reasons it could also be argued that slavery had been assumed not explicitly allowed at least in Common Law pre-1791. Many States would deny this. They would say it was not only Customary Law but had been in US Federal Law. But was that true? If they said (for instance) 'The 1788 Constitution was meant only for US citizens' the answer then is − 'How then is coercive power and unchecked authority legitimate over anyone else?' At the least to claim such power and authority was morally wrong. It was arrogance.

And −

(a) the Federal Government in theory drew its authority from the US Constitution;

(b) The Bill of Rights seems − in Articles IV and V − opposed to coercive power.

(Note that one main reason such exploitation of US citizens was not allowed was precisely because they were <u>persons</u>.)

Chapter 8

The 1788 Constitution mentions 'the year 1808': the reason being that it aimed to stop the importation of slaves to the USA in that year. (In fact this happened in 1809.) But before 1809 the US importation of slaves was vast! Hundreds of thousands even between 1780 and 1809.

In 1807 William Wilberforce, after years of intense struggle, persuaded Parliament to abolish the slave trade in British territories. Then the Royal Navy was charged with eradicating the trade on the seas and the British colonies. This did not, legally, abolish slavery as such (as noted above). We should notice that even though 1807, 1808 and 1809 were years of some progress in the USA and Britain, we must always distinguish conceptually between enslavement and the many slave trades. Enslavement involves a process, or act, or series of acts, of making someone a slave. [This is actually a chattel slave – someone treated as property by an 'owner' and deprived of legal (and, in effect, of human) rights.] A slave trade is in organised traffic in such 'slaves' – with the evil intention of selling them.

Slavery is the state (usually enforced by law) of being someone's property and under his direction and – even more important! – a life-long captive (unless emancipated), subject to arbitrary and very, very cruel punishments! Indeed – as Kenneth Stampp implies – slavery in the Deep South was a fate far worse than death! He says that slaves in some States would prefer death!

A slave was (usually) divested of all of his birth family and – if possible even crueller – often divested of his own wife (or husband) and children! He or she was 'owned', forced to labor, subject to (many) punishments, could not move freely (e.g. because 'slave patrols' might hunt him or her), could not enjoy the fruits of his toil and was (rigidly) excluding from political society – and participation. As Booker Washington states – and as Edward Bates' family proved –

some (perhaps numerically a fair number of slave-owners in the period 1775 to 1865) were not vicious people. Yet vicious owners were common. Slavery was always an affront to human dignity – even when it was not in practice cruel by the standards of the time – which were (very) far below what is now considered humane.

Chapter 9

So it is hard – sometimes not possible – to imagine a crueller lifelong condition than chattel slavery! To wish to 'escape' is both a human reaction and may be one required by common sense – though taking into account that conditions might get worse if caught! That is a reason why a so-called 'Fugitive Slave Clause' is one of the cruellest 'legal' devices imaginable. No wonder no Framer of either Constitution dared to describe it in plain language in either US Constitution.

Yet – even taking into account that neither US Constitution anywhere defines 'free person' or 'unfree person' still less 'slave' (which it never uses or mentions!), a 'Fugitive Slave Clause' was the interpretation placed on paragraph 3 of Section 2 of Article IV! Such a provision was almost as cruel as judicial use of torture! But (ignoring or overlooking this) most US lawyers and citizens took it as Federal Law as it was in the text of the Constitution(s). They had reason! Could it be denied the Constitution was 'Supreme Law' of the USA? And did not the Supreme Court 'recognise' US slavery? (In the *Dred Scott v. Sandford* case implying that slaves were property!)

However even one reading of paragraphs 1, 2 and 3 of Article IV of the 1788 Constitution at once shows that paragraph 3 is:

(i)   radically new; and
(ii) so badly drafted that it can be abused;
(iii) gives abusive power to 'claimants'. Firstly they can activate agents to violently 'give back' a slave – secondly the slave can then be severely punished. Was it a function of a Constitution dedicated to liberty (for citizens) to give anyone abusive power?

The apparently 'legal' language of paragraph 3 bewitched even great US lawyers (for instance Abraham Lincoln for most of his career. In the 1840s, we are told, he represented in Court a (slave-claiming) 'party' – even though Lincoln always held slavery to be evil).

It is vital to see that the language was 'legalese' – not well drafted and careful language appropriate to a National Constitution. We need ask only – how was a 'fugitive (slave) to be 'delivered up' exactly? By capture and violence. To his, or her 'owner'. Yet the clause contains no such part! Was it then to 'the party' who claimed him? But the clause says only that labor 'may' be due to such a party! More important still in what condition is the fugitive to be? Injured or healthy? Alive or dead? Even this is not in the clause! Though a lawful Constitutional provision should not allow death or injury! And who legally might lay hands on the 'fugitive slave'? So far as the words go – anyone – and with no restraint on violence!! Indeed in many cases it was not 'the party' who did so but a cruel hired agent. Also they – the party or the agent – could kidnap free 'blacks' – one was Stanhope who spent 14 years in Southern slavery.

The questions in the last paragraph above demolish the idea that the clause could be either well-drafted or in accord with The Declaration of Independence – let alone fair or humane!.

Also note, as Jacobus Ten Broek points out, that the clause contains no grant of powers to Congress! Indeed, contradicts the Preamble to the US Constitution (e.g. establishing justice!) as it implies powers of kidnap and violence be used to 'deliver up' slaves – and those mistaken for slaves! How else could a 'fugitive' slave be delivered up?

In effect the clause encourages either 'household violence' or 'street violence' or 'group violence' – and if the slave resists strongly – 'extreme bodily injury'! Also, the clause ignores the offense to ordinary US people e.g. in Massachusetts and Vermont and New York. Also a natural consequence of The Fugitive Slave as usually interpreted, though not a necessary consequence, was: that it was a licence to practice cruelty! So ordinary people could be not only offended but outraged.

Very many slave-owners regarded their slaves as human 'property' and the slave might be whipped or badly flogged for trying to 'escape', or even – as happened to Alex Haley's ancestor – mutilated. Alex Haley, in *Roots* tells us Kunta Kinte had a limb cut off for repeated

23

attempts to 'escape'. That was in 'Colonial' days – but the author of *Hard Trials on My Way* (J. A. Scott) quotes the memory of a former US 'slave' who said her 'master' would not lash slaves – but could kill a slave. He was generally not at all cruel – just (occasionally?), willing to kill one!

Some people may however say that The Fugitive Slave Clause – as usually interpreted – could be mild – for instance could the slave not be 'delivered up' by coach to 'the party'? Possibly – given an armed guard in the coach! Violence was inherent in seizing and forcible deporting men – and women with children – many hundreds of miles (often the slaves were in ragged clothes unsuited to any weather – sometimes chained).

Those who wrote these words thought little of their history! Jesus had been delivered for trial, then for mockery, then for scourging – and then delivered up for Crucifixion! So, The Fugitive Slave Clause unconsciously displayed the facts that thousands and thousands of 'negroes' (not all slaves) were to be delivered to huge sufferings – as Jesus had been. His was the Passion of Christ – theirs was the Passion of the chained, flogged and lonely 'slave'.

Chapter 10

So our questions now become specifically:

(1) Did the 1788 US Constitution legalise chattel slavery in the USA? Or recognise it? It was universally – and truly – held that it allowed it. But was it Constitutional?

(2) Did the 1791 Amended US Constitution do so? Did Article IV Section 2 (paragraph 3) have any claim on 'slaves'? How could it, given its sloppy terms? Granted it was Customary Law.

(3) Did the year 1809 signify a large change in the practice of having slaves in the US States? (This last question is answered at once: No – slavery increased greatly!)

It has often been argued that Washington and Jefferson:

(a) wished to confine slavery to States where it already existed in 1775 to 1778;

(b) aimed and intended that it should die out but by a gradual process! Not by interference with laws and practices in the States. Parts of the correspondence of Washington and Jefferson support this view. But there are major objections to it! Is there evidence that either man intended to do in practice what was necessary to end slavery effectively – even by a gradual process – whatever that was? Washington said in a letter he wished slavery abolished by law – but, as President, did not refuse to sign the 1793 Fugitive Slave Act! He thus entrenched slavery by law! Moreover, much earlier neither man had strenuously fought (to the last gasp) against Pierce Butler's idea of a (slave-holding) Federal Union.

A man should not be held for life to positions he may have

inherited. Nevertheless Washington was both a land owner and a slave owner on a huge scale!

His biographer, Esmond Wright [*Washington and the American Revolution* (English University Press, 1937, page 36, also Penguin, 1973], says:

'In January 1759 then Washington added to his own 5,000 acres and 49 slaves the wealth of the Custis plantation, 17,000 acres, a fortune set at £23,000, some 300 slaves and a town house in the colonial capital at Williamsburg . . . ' (My italics)

Wright further tells us – in a passage that is incredible, even if it only reflects Wright's own distaste for Washington's business practices (page 39):

'By 1772 Washington was shipping 270 barrels of flour to the West Indies too, rather 'musty' flour he confessed, but it would permit the buying of slaves if 'choice ones' could be got for less than £40 a head!' (My italics)

If the words Wright quote came from Washington a state of mind is revealed that is venal and inhuman! But if they are Wright's own words, he has no business putting them in a passage on Washington. Or are they meant to be the words of some agent who will get 'choice slaves' for 'musty flour'?

We must always remember – an important fact sometimes forgotten – that slavery was abolished much earlier in the nineteenth century in 'British' territories than it was in the USA! (The Parliamentary 'abolition' only had full effect in the West Indies in 1838.) However, it is the record of the USA in regard to the 1788 – and then the 1791 – Constitution which concerns us. Did Federal Law recognise slavery in the Constitution(s)? We saw the years 1788 and 1791 and the years 1807, 1808, and 1809 are all important in the history of action against the slave trade. But that does not stop (US) slavery! We have seen that – on one reading of the 1791 Constitution (which I argue for) – *The Bill of Rights* of 1791 – directly contradicted the 'legality' of (all) US slavery. (Unless the slave had been convicted of a major crime by jury trial.) Yet a form of words was devised which most lawyers applied to 'fugitive slaves'. But Alvan Stewart rightly held it null and void of authority!

Chapter 11

We saw that it would be unjust to hold Washington for life to views be held before or in 1772. But on the other hand we should not ignore Robert Harvey's evidence [in *A Few Bloody Noses*. John Murray (page 360)], that – incredible as it may seem! Washington did not think one of his female slaves worked hard enough! It was not on Washington's radar, then, that he owned and kept (any) slaves very unjustly, and worked them very unjustly! He could deprive them of the leisure he enjoyed – his opulence derived in part from the labor of others! He was (Harvey tells us) an exacting master in regard to hard work for all his slaves. Such views and acts entrench slavery – rather than 'gradually diminish' it! No doubt very many others did the same – but they were not a General then President of the USA. Many, many slaveholders were not rich and owned only a few slaves. They were not near Washington's scale and social position.

Since Washington had, even by 1772, for long enjoyed a great military reputation and social position in Virginia, we can dismiss the argument that he had to follow prevailing social customs in regard to slaves. Not so. Action from Washington could have freed many slaves – and might have led to the freeing of many more by other 'owners'. He might well have incurred enmity – but hardly ostracism. He was far too formidable for that. Jefferson was likely to take his part also. It is true that Robert Harvey also states (*A Few Bloody Noses,* page 360), that in 1786 Washington privately expressed the view:

'*There is not a man living who wishes more sincerely than I do to see a plan adopted for the gradual abolition of it . . . it being along my first wishes to see some means adopted by which slavery may be abolished by law . . .*' (My italics)

Washington wished this state of affairs to come about. Yet he knew existing US slavery was wrong. And in 1785 he (had) refused to sign a petition for the Abolition of slavery! Nor would he even publicly give hospitality to a (lady) slave writer who contacted him! He wished for the Abolition of slavery by law. This suggests a more radical set of moves than the 'gradual abolition' he talks of in his first sentence. Yet he neither sponsored nor advanced laws to get rid of slavery! Indeed, as President, he signed the First 'Fugitive Slave' Act! So in 1793 he certainly allowed slavery to continue by law – very openly and explicitly. He perpetuated it by law! He ensured by his act that it would harshly control – in fact seize and transport – slaves who 'escaped'.

His actions cancelled his wishes. They continued the enslavement of many and the capture and 'delivering up' of fugitive slaves! True, when it came to his death, he emancipated all his slaves. But during his life his pace was slow. (This, by the way, was not unusual for him – he only seems to have decided to act for Independence at some point between 1764 and 1770.) For nearly all his adult life he had ample opportunities to emancipate many slaves. And no American – not even Franklin – was better placed or regarded than he. He could have persuaded many to free slaves. Jefferson, Samuel Adams, and Washington had all made many criticisms of tyranny – and what was slave-holding but a cruel inhuman tyranny? Washington was not simply inconsistent. He was an official upholder of slavery as of 1793! Yet he had much earlier stated it held "tame and abject 'blacks'" by arbitrary sway.

There is a contradiction – (not just a tension) – between Washington's slave-holding and his will to free American citizens from (British) 'tyranny'. Some of Washington's slaves may have had forbears who were Americans before his own. All his slaves were tyrannised over – not brutally but by the insidious power that – in his own words – made (black) slaves abject! All US slaves were held by acts of tyranny – originated by British slave-traders to enslave (innocent) men, women and children by brute force. The use was often in one sense passive – in that some Americans took it for granted they could have slaves.

Yet often the use was active. Some Americans bought slaves and sold them. We are told that Jefferson and Washington both sold slaves.

If this is true – (and I personally have not seen real evidence of this) – then words would fail me.

For what have economic motives to say against – when it is in a person's power – dismantling a tyranny. Granted many – and probably most – Southern slave-owners did sincerely not think slave-owning a tyranny. But the almost unanimous witness of observers who travelled in the South – [for instance Frederick Law Olmsted, Williamand Frances Seward and Fanny Kemble (a British observer)] is decisively that slaves were treated with and by tyranny. Consider e.g. any account of slave-sicknesses.

Chapter 12

Washington's caution in regard to freeing all his slaves was more tragic than could be imagined! Even as a young man he could have freed and resettled his own slaves. He had very ample land. He was also a friend of Lord Fairfax's son. The Privy Council (stupidly!) decided that Lord Fairfax owned much more than three million acres! Washington – who had surveying skills – could have asked Lord Fairfax outright to settle very many slaves as free men on Lord Fairfax's land. This was reasonable and needed no bravery. It was not even an act that required unusual energy.

When Washington did fight for Independence, and was a General, he could have proclaimed 'freedom' for slaves who fought as soldiers – (on the side of Independence). By contrast, Washington was furious when a Loyalist Governor (Lord Dunmore), proclaimed freedom for slaves (who fought on the Loyalist side!). But Washington did – to his credit – ask Congress to give slaves a role in the army. When Washington was President he could – and certainly should – have stated publicly he opposed all slavery. Even in 1791 he could have stated publicly that The Bill of Rights was incompatible with all US slavery. Or – if he did not believe this – he could well have asked the Framers to put in another paragraph which banned slavery in the United States. And (as we have seen) he could have refused to sign the 1793 'Fugitive Slave Act'! In fact, given his principles, he must have opposed even the idea of such an act – if his principles were as he stated! Something was very badly wrong with his thinking and his actions.

It is not enough to reply: in the case of any of those actions the Southern States would have seceded! There is literal truth in this. In the case of public and official action against slavery some or all Southern delegates would have at least protested a lot in Congress. And they might have left it. Perhaps they would have acted to make a Southern Republic. But nearly all Northern slaves could have been emancipated and some Southern ones (e.g. Jefferson's and Washington's). Had some Southern States wanted a war, they might have had no prospect of winning it. And how would they trade without a navy? And if Washington (either as General or President – or both) called militias and planned an army who would or could defeat it?

It will be rightly said this would have begun a time of anarchy. Frankly, this might have happened. But much would have depended on how strongly Washington and allies were seen to act so as to dissociate the Union from all slavery. Washington could have acted very strongly. He had a duty not to usher in anarchy. But had he not also a greater duty to make it clear the Union would not tolerate generations of enslavement? Also, would many Southern Statesmen have even risked enmity with Washington e.g. when President? Was he not both far too formidable both as President and – if he wished – (again) as General? (He had sometimes quelled debate in Congress much earlier by a single remark!) For instance he was famous across the Union for his ability to overcome all setbacks.

Perhaps a viable arrangement would have been to make 1793 the year in which the President gave a State of the Union message in which he said all owners were asked to emancipate slaves, to show their patriotism and a belief in the principles of the Declaration of Independence. Naturally this would have had to be accompanied with, or include, statements saying the President thought the proposed Fugitive Slave Act (of 1793) unwise: he could have added that Article IV of the 1791 US Constitution was already in place. So, as well as being unwise, a new Act was unnecessary! Indeed it would – (or at least might) – cause hostility and boycotts by foreign nations. Also a far-sighted statesman could have seen it would make more likely a Civil War. This might have put the onus of opposing public opinion on slave owners without generating anarchy or war. (It would also incidentally have caused some reflective people to ask whether The Fugitive Slave Clause made sense.)

However, as regards (even) a gradual death of slavery in the United States, Washington was a total failure! His strong wish never became an effective plan let alone completed action! At least – if he had an effective plan it was not activated in his lifetime.

There is something hugely unjust in Washington as landowner saying his slaves should work and then work. Why? For whom? If for Washington's family, his estates, his business and his projects, then this is sheer exploitation! (even if the 'slaves' are given reasonable food, housing, and leisure, and Sunday time for worship). It does not need a Karl Marx to note the exploitation of forced labor and the 'surplus value' accruing to the owner and his family.

When we come to Washington as General there is further injustice! Washington deserves great credit for trying to get Congress to give some role to slaves fleeing to the cause of troops fighting for US Independence. But he also asked Congress to increase the number of lashes his soldiers might get for serious offences! (This was not fair or humane.)

However it is true that the British Army was prone to far worse abuse of soldiers who seriously offended. Washington's practice was much better than British ones. Robert Harvey tells us that one American under a previous British command had received five hundred lashes! The same man was later in an American campaign against Canada! (He must have had superhuman strength.)

John Adams, a contemporary, tells us that Washington was very modest but had a high sense of social position (e.g. his own)! This sense may have been an obstacle to liberty for all in the New Republic – by lessening his sense of the rights of all inhabitants – slaves and 'Indians' included.

Chapter 13

Social position is not the same as caste – which is far more rigid and constraining in societies which recognise it. But when social position is believed to necessarily exclude people who, for instance, earn a bare living with the work of their hands and – still more – slaves, it has a similar function and effect to caste.

In that looser sense slaves were the victims of a social barrier as rigid as caste. It is true they could be emancipated. It is also true that even in the early US Republic there had been some 'free blacks'. But a view was in many circles and in most classes prevalent that 'negroes' were not able to match 'white men' for either intelligence or civilisation – and that they were more fit for hard labor! Such non-factual assumptions often contributed to a segregation which in effect was a kind of caste system – at least in the way it rigidly resisted any idea of 'whites' and 'blacks' as equals – still less as inherently equal as regards (US) citizenship . . . ('Free blacks' were not necessarily US citizens – though some were.)

This anti-factual bias ignored the very terrible conditions in which 'black' ancestors had been stolen and transported on slave-ships (and then sold). It even ignored the almost equally terrible way many of these people were 'broken' into a slave way of life. And it ignored the way generations of slaves were brutally treated. For instance some were hanged in smokehouses!

No factual inquiry could at the time eradicate a habit of mind which had been 'aired' by so many and for a long time in North America. It had come before the USA and was widespread in the USA. The reader is owed a demarcation of the two ideas of 'caste' and 'class'. Each terms has several meanings – but for the purposes of this study of 'slaves' (the) respective (main) ones are:

Caste

An hereditary, rigid and usually enforced, division of ranked status in a society – such that each rank is taken to have common activities and common features – but does not mix with ranks 'lower in a scale'. (There may be a group or class of no caste – lower than any ranked one and deemed 'untouchable'. Hence, caste systems often implicitly or explicitly embody ideas of 'purity' and (by contrast) 'uncleanliness' of untouchables.)

Class

An economic or socially specified group of people (which may be very large, large or small) in a society whose income and assets (if any) derive from control of land, or raw materials, or animals, or human work, or means of transport – and which may have varying or (more rarely), fixed membership and which derives some powers (and often great power) from its de facto control of such resources or assets.

By analogy with this – but less centrally – a class may also be a group of people socially specified by access to education or (probably more often), by access to training in arms or in (military or other) leadership roles. An economist – (or a sociologist – or for that matter any Marxist) – may tighten up my rough accounts of how caste and class differ. But it will be a guide to have the two accounts before us as we see in further chapters how US slavery could be thought of in both ways – even though they are distinct.

For instance – slave-labor was both exploited (by a class – indeed by several) – but also was quite often thought of as the work of people so low in a scale they were like 'untouchables'. For instance any white person – even a child! – might challenge any black person in many Southern States.

Chapter 14

Land was an aim of most Americans. Even men of property aimed high. For instance Washington had a desire to acquire more and more land! This appears at all stages of his career! Esmond Wright points out that this practice had already taken hold among North American settlers more than a century before Washington – and been roundly condemned by Roger Taylor. But Washington was a man of great wealth and had no need of the thousands of acres he added to his estates from time to time. At birth Washington had land – at his marriage he acquired far more (having already much. Later he got 24,000 acres more!)

Wright points out that (to his credit) it was Washington who moved the Virginia authorities to make grants of land to ex-soldiers. This would have been truly impressive had Washington not been granted 24,000 acres of (this) land for himself! (Wright tells us it might have been less had some soldiers not been without money!) Given Washington's circumstances his example was a bad one: he could have given very much of his land to poor soldiers. And to his own slaves – and those of others if they emancipated them.

Washington seems to have been addicted to acquiring land. Yet he was in a good position to know that land is a subtle, and some-times agile, cause of disputes, opulence, war, and border-raids. Not to mention the fact that the poor, slaves and 'Indians' were entitled to some land also! (Since many Indians had been divested of 'tribal' lands.) Some poor people in the South had hardly any or no land.

Washington (could and) should from 1760 on have divested him-self of some of his estates. He could have benefited thousands of slaves (later also those soldiers whose poverty deprived them of land!). Why did he not do so? The longer his career, and the prestige it generated, lasted the greater the opportunity. But Washington left a void where he should have demonstrated responsibility and the resolute response to horrendous odds which his military career had shown.

We must give space and credit to Washington's good wishes to abolish slavery. I must have the charity to say they expressed long term intentions. However, Washington's conduct as landowner, as General and as President as regards slaves seems inert (though he did emancipate his slaves finally).

Washington may have had a blindness as to the (great) need for quick social change (e.g. in the South). Perhaps he as statesman thought that only a transition which preserved a class-based order would preserve the Union? Robert Harvey, for instance, argues that a (gentry) class 'tamed' the American Revolution by, in practice, imposing a settlement less favourable to democracy than could have arisen. (Not of course the gentry who favoured retaining British allegiance. These emigrated to Canada or were dispossessed – often both.)

It is a tenable and reasonable view that the USA had to retain a class system from 1775 on – so that the Federal Government had officials. But even so had Washington had the moral foresight to free his slaves by 1775 the good effect of his actions could have helped the Union's statesmanship – as well as giving a jolt to his class to emancipate slaves. He might have been a paradigm for (most) US citizens – at least in the North, parts of Virginia, Maryland – and later, the West.

Even in a class-based order Washington should have divested himself of some land – and (at once) freed his slaves. As we saw they could have made a living on his (former) land. True, this would have been very unusual at the time and hugely unpopular (in most Southern States). But it was almost precisely what he said was his intention.

Harvey thinks Washington one of the greatest men in history. Lincoln thought Washington should be thought of as 'a perfect man'. I cannot agree with either judgement! Washington had courage, prudence, iron self-control, fortitude, decisive judgement, a sense of duty, and he was a great patriot and leader, (though not a General of the record or genius of Lee or Grant), and was a statesman central to all US life of his time and since. He was a model of courage in adversity!

But – to take only two examples of problems in his judgement – his small regard for the thought behind the 'Proclamation Line' of 1769, which protected some Indian lands – or, more exactly, would have done so had it been respected and observed – was very unwise. Also should Washington have been confident that a larger standing army and more centralised laws and power (in a Federal Government), made US citizens freer than under the British Crown – which had usually not kept a standing army in the Colonies? Why was not the plan, advocated by Joseph Galloway, whereby Americans would have freedom but retain the Crown and a place in the Empire not properly considered? This was, it appears to me, a far better option for US prosperity and emancipation – which would have come much sooner! As Robert Harvey points out access to the most extensive and efficient trade network in the world was hugely beneficial to American Freedom(s) and could go with it. (Even the freedom to live under written law.) Note again the beneficial consequences to America had Lord Chief Justice Mansfield's judgment of 1772 been taken as a precedent to free American slaves because slavery was not recognised in (British) law. Had American law followed British law – as it possibly might have under Galloway's plan – much American slavery could have ended by 1793. Washington could have aided this process by freeing his slaves and praising Franklin's anti-slavery work. And stating his belief in equal liberty for all US residents (e.g. slaves and 'Indians'.) This point may be Utopian – was there not far too much prejudice against both slaves and Indians? Yet Washington could still have indicated a different point of view – even if only in speeches.

Chapter 15

Washington had already explicitly recognised, on August 24, 1774, (see David Reynolds: *America, Empire of Liberty* (Allen Lane, Penguin Imprint, 2009, page 61 and especially note 8, page 602); that US slavery was arbitrary, exploitative and (morally) wrong! His exact words (to 'his brother-in-law in Virginia' as David Reynolds gives them) being:

> '. . . the Crisis is arrived when we must assert our Rights or Submit to every Imposition than can be heaped upon us till custom and use will make us as tame and abject slaves as the Blacks we Rule over with such arbitrary sway.' (My italics)

This is one of the most important admissions ever made in history! The word 'abject' is especially important. It rules out – by definition – that countervailing reasons can justify – let alone morally justify – treatment (by anyone), which reduces a human being to such a condition. As for the person doing it: to claim to be an 'Owner' or 'Master' of slaves highlights the injustice! (And such 'owners' employ cruel overseers.) Washington 'ruled over' 'blacks'. But humanity does not depend on colour of skin or origin or any country or continent. (To recognise he was one of many slave-owners does not make the inhumanity less.) This is a truth Jefferson explicitly saw – and Congress implied when sponsoring The Declaration of Independence.

So Washington recognised that 'rule' over slaves was arbitrary, despotic, (since it gave unjust power to 'owners' and their agents), and was so unjust as to make the slaves 'abject' – yet he did not at once, emancipate his slaves or try to change State or Federal laws – despite this being his intention! His intention did not govern his action!

One obstacle was perhaps his and others (sincere) beliefs – i.e. that 'negroes' were less able than 'whites' – though (contradictory to this!)

somehow more able for hard labor. An even vaster and, if possible, cruder obstacle was the sheer mass-power of many – (taken together) – in the slave-owning classes. This was daily apparent not only in 'slave laws' (in some States), but in cruel 'overseers', and in punishments and 'slave patrols'. Words may not quite express the sheer force of power exerted daily against slaves – by conditions of labor, punishment, inadequate food, restraints of various kinds, State laws (of course) – even dogs to hunt 'runaways'.

Could anyone have abated that force by words? Strange as it may seem I would say: Yes. Congress could, to some extent Washington could – if for instance he had given a speech as President on the issue.

Chapter 16

To, willingly and intentionally, tolerate treatment which makes any human being 'a tame and abject slave' is to injure his or her human condition. A human being can feel – (specifically can have many, many kinds of feelings) – and also be aware of his or her conditions and wish to change them. Such facts make abjection inhuman – a pervasive invasion of the (many kinds of) feelings and intentions people are entitled (as human) to enjoy. Anyone who denies that shows that his or her idea of what constitutes humanity is not accurate.

It may be said that prevailing human customs do not always allow some persons to treat some slaves otherwise. But this was not the case in regard to many British or American slave-owners. (It applied not at all to Washington, or to many other rich US 'owners'. Rich slave-holders could have got a living with no slaves!) It is true – and I fully accept this – that some US slave-holders would have been persecuted and perhaps some murdered if they emancipated their own 'slaves'. (Possibly – though this is a little doubtful – the same would have happened to some ('owners') if they simply treated their 'slaves' as if they were free.) Nevertheless – by Washington's own admission and his principles – the onus was on him to emancipate his slaves. For instance, he had admitted to arbitrary sway over tame and abject 'blacks'.

US customs in many States (Southern – and New Jersey) would have made fair and humane treatment of 'slaves' very hard. Some 'owners' would have met suffering when they openly gave much improved treatment to their slaves. In the South social law, habit and custom were a kind of tyranny. But could they have prevented rich slave-owners from changing their ways so that 'slaves' were emancipated and given a job?

An important conceptual point which implies a major moral criticism of all such slave-owners is that they did not examine and act on the issue – what are the natural and necessary consequences of enslaving a person? This conceptual point was made very forcibly by J. F. Maxwell in his critical account of the (deplorable) record of the Catholic Church in regard to slavery (for over a thousand years!). (There were also ways in which the Church fought to abate slavery. The record was not all of one kind.)

'Slave-owners' however often used Christian texts to encourage submission of slaves. This was both base and predictably so – another example of class ideology being pushed out and onto the powerless. The natural and necessary consequences of enslaving someone are – among other things – that he is under pressure to behave immaturely – perhaps childishly – and to butter up his 'owner' – to lose manly or womanly dignity – and perhaps self-respect. And to work less if possible – which, given punishments by overseers, was often not possible.

Chapter 17

A critic may say: 'You (the writer) have nearly contradicted yourself! You say The Fugitive Slave Clause was clearly Unconstitutional, (even though in the texts of 1788 and 1791), but you also say (all) slaves were without power. Yet slaves could in a few cases have asked some Abolitionist lawyer to argue they were Constitutionally freed – e.g. by Article IV of The Bill of Rights'.

My answer to this is: 'In pure theory you are quite right. But almost every Southern State Court would if it heard a case at all just have said' – (in the person of the Judge):

'This Court is not even required by Federal – still less State law – to hear you at all, because –

(a) you go against State law; and
(b) the Supreme Court – as well as the 1791 Constitution itself – admits both State laws and The Fugitive Slave Clause as both Constitutional and so legally both paramount and sound.'

The Abolitionist lawyer would then have been dismissed from the Court.

A Federal Court (before at earliest 1858) would probably have said:

'Your case and client have – as the State Court implied – no standing to bring a case.'

Also any slave had almost no chance of getting a good lawyer.

Chapter 18

US slavery implied power of the owner – to keep the slave subservient, to punish him (e.g. for 'escaping'). True there could have been some improvement in the conditions of many 'slaves'. For example – all punishments could have been banned (by laws or rules) and the working hours made less. No sales away from wife or husband (or of children away from parents) should ever have been made. All this was consistent with US views on rights! It could, for instance, have been enacted by (either or both) Congress and (many) State legislatures. (Washington could, at least, have gone as far as Jefferson and Franklin in trying to get Congress to condemn slavery.) Concise legal reasoning, if repeated in Congress, could have added a real pursuit of a better life for slaves – by pointing out, that humans respond best not to punishment but rewards. (The fortitude, bravery and empathy of slaves were met by very harsh treatment.)

It is true economic factors may have seemed on the side of Southern slave-holders. Their crops might have stopped (without enough laborers). As Clinton Rossiter points out 'free labor' could often ask for a higher wage than in England. [In some Southern States this may not have held (where laborers were very poor)]. On the other hand if reforms had been officially sponsored (by Congress in liaison with some States) it is not impossible that some 'free' 'black' laborers might have chosen to work in plantation areas. No doubt they would have needed new incentives!

These economic factors – as André Meyer has pointed out – weighed very heavily at the time on the side of the status quo. I must not paint a picture of the probability of either much emancipation or even paid 'slave' laborers with improved conditions . . . My point has to be rather than given a great deal of powerful sponsorship by e.g. Federal agencies, many specific improvements in poor slave conditions were not impossible.

Washington admits that it is '. . . *(the) Blacks we Rule over with such arbitrary sway*'! (My italics). He thereby admits that the practice of ('owners') having slaves is not a contract but a matter of 'Ruling over' people – i.e. violating their free will by not allowing it to have free scope! The 'Rule' is neither democratic nor rational. It is an 'Arbitrary Sway'! (Washington did not use a capital letter for 'arbitrary (sway)' – yet the concept is one that is condemned by his own words.) The 'Rule' is not best or for the best – still less the result of choice of what is morally good over what is less good or not good – rather the 'Rule' results from 'Arbitrary Sway', (as well as greed, blindness to humanity, racialism, exploitation, and other evils). He tacitly grants Maxwell's point – that slaves are made less than they are – they are demeaned and sometimes infantilised. Their free will, initiative, industriousness and daily work are degraded by not allowing their integrity to act. (Many slaves of course acted with great dignity and self-control under such a regime.)

I am not saying each slave-owner had all such evil motives: I am saying that the fact that the 'Sway' was arbitrary and applied to people described in terms of colour of skin imposed no barrier to venal slave-holders and their punishments! And these punishments were very savage! Indeed, a moment's thought should have convinced State legislatures that no-one has a right to punish anyone savagely!

I am not accusing Washington of being venal: I am saying that to impose forced labor on his slaves was exploitation. (Consider for instance a reversal of role – labor being exacted from Washington as a slave. That would also have been exploitation.) And I am accusing him of a culpable lack of attention to the consequences of his enslave-ments! Not only him – many others were harsher to their slaves.

Whether Washington thought slavery was less important than 'America's rights' – a very grave misjudgement in itself! Or whether he consciously 'looked away' from American slavery (as it was), because he realised its iniquity and did not have the moral courage to face and eliminate these evils (e.g. from 1780 on) I don't know. Perhaps he was, previously, so 'caught up' in making an army that he had to let alone serious duties to those inhumanly treated – slaves in particular. In any case America's greatest 'hero' was unheroic in this area – at least that is what seems true on the evidence known to me (given his express intention to gradually abolish US slavery).

I grant that Washington had to keep a sharp eye out, that e.g. Virginia, South and North Carolina, did not leave the Union. (This would have been serious.) He cannot be criticised for wishing to keep them in and for doing things to keep them in. (Even possibly – though this is doubtful – for saying neither emancipation nor changing State laws need be immediate – only quite soon – e.g. by 1808). But note that Pierce Butler of South Carolina kept slaves so abject they were literally laid down sick to death in his 'infirmary'. (Fanny Kemble records this point). So at least action to help slaves was the greater priority.

Chapter 19

Washington admits that it is ' . . . *(the) Blacks we Rule over with such arbitrary sway'*! (My italics) He thereby admits that the practice of ('owners') having slaves is not a contract but a matter of 'Ruling over' people – i.e. violating their free will by not allowing it to have free scope! The 'Rule' is neither democratic nor rational. It is an 'Arbitrary Sway'! (Washington did not use a capital letter for 'arbitrary (sway)' – yet the concept is one that is condemned by his own words.) The 'Rule' is not best or for the best – still less the result of choice of what is morally good over what is less good or not good – rather the 'Rule' results from 'Arbitrary Sway', (as well as greed, blindness to humanity, racialism, exploitation, and other evils). He tacitly grants Maxwell's point – that slaves are made less than they are – they are demeaned and sometimes infantilised. Their free will, initiative, industriousness and daily work are degraded by not allowing their integrity to act. (Many slaves of course acted with great dignity and self-control under such a regime.)

I am not saying each slave-owner had all such evil motives: I am saying that the fact that the 'Sway' was arbitrary and applied to people described in terms of colour of skin imposed no barrier to venal slave-holders and their punishments! And these punishments were very savage!

I am not accusing Washington of being venal: I am saying that to impose forced labor on his slaves was exploitation. (Consider for instance a reversal of role – labor being exacted from Washington as a slave. That would also have been exploitation.) And I am accusing him of a culpable lack of attention to the conseq uences of his enslavements! Not only him – many others were harsher to their slaves.

Whether Washington thought slavery was less important than 'America's rights' – a very grave misjudgement in itself! Or whether he consciously 'looked away' from American slavery (as it was), because he realised its iniquity and did not have the moral courage to face and eliminate these evils (e.g. from 1780 on) I don't know. Perhaps he was, previously, so 'caught up' in making an army that he had to let alone serious duties to those inhumanly treated – slaves in particular. In any case America's greatest 'hero' was unheroic in this area – at least that is what seems true on the evidence known to me (given his express intention to gradually abolish US slavery).

I grant that Washington had to keep a sharp eye out, that e.g. Virginia, South and North Carolina, did not leave the Union. (This would have been serious.) He cannot be criticised for wishing to keep them in and for doing things to keep them in. (Even possibly – though this is doubtful – for saying neither emancipation nor changing State laws need be immediate – only quite soon – e.g. by 1808). We saw that Pierce Butler of South Carolina kept slaves so abject they were literally laid down sick to death in his 'infirmary'. (Fanny Kemble records this point.) So at least action to help slaves was the greater priority.

Chapter 20

It is hardly credible – yet true – that paragraph 3 of Article IV of both US Constitutions (i.e. 'The Fugitive Slave Clause') was formulated so that any 'party' might claim anyone whom he believed had 'escaped' as his slave!! (When the 'party' made a claim there was no rigorous check on the person he claimed at the time even though he or she could have been a US citizen.) Free 'blacks' were sometimes 'delivered up' to Southern slave-owners. And the families of 'escaped' slaves. The children might be very young and their mother ill or desperate for their freedom! The claimant might be wicked and cruel. Yet his mere claim was not illegal – even if in the end a Magistrate (in a 'Free State' for example) might not approve it.

Legally the party's 'claim' did not have to be considered by a Court or a jury! (As we saw) it was sometimes considered by a Magistrate. Nor did the 'slave' have to be taken to a Court. The 'service' or 'labor' might not be – and sometimes was not – 'due' to the 'party'. Nor – a very crucial point – was the 'party' or his agent made to stop if aware of 'Free' State Laws. This violates paragraph 1 of Article IV – which enjoins respect for the laws of (Free) States. It violates it by the lack of respect for the freedoms in 'Free States'.

The 'delivery' often involved violence. This often led to great cruelty (e.g. to women seized by 'slave-hunters'). As we have just implied, it was often also specifically illegal violence – contrary to legal presumptions in 'Free States'! (In Vermont it was contrary to State law).

Note the four-fold inhumanity:

(a) an unjustly enslaved person was said to 'escape';
(b) could be 'claimed' and treated with violence;
(c) was again enslaved – often with more violence (also to his family on occasion);

49

(d) could then be punished to the point of death – and arbitrarily! (The punishment(s) were at the 'party's' will.) If the slave 'delivered' back to the 'party' lived after punishment (and most did – we believe) he or she could always be punished more later!

Chapter 21

Chattel slavery implies both captivity and forced labor! The very wording of paragraph 3 states that what 'may be due' (to a 'party') under State law(s) is service or labor and not slavery! Both service and labor are initiated by the worker not the 'owner'. 'The party' is even less relevant – since he was not always by State law 'due' service or labor – he might just be mistaken!

Also I concede the plain fact that paragraph 3 of Article IV is part of the texts of the US Constitutions of 1788 and 1791. This proves only that paragraph 3 was aimed at certain 'fugitives', not that it achieved a part of the US Supreme Law. It did not do so (I argue) because – among other reasons – 'the party' could have been a (released) criminal and a congenital liar. Also, as we have just seen, it encouraged contravening paragraph 1 of Article IV by its brutal lack of respect for the (legal) freedoms and laws of Free States!

There is a logical gap between requiring some persons who 'may' be 'due' to give 'service or labor' to be 'delivered up' and requiring all so-called 'fugitive slaves' to be – by force – 'delivered up' because of (unchecked) 'claims' by 'parties'! The persons claimed may not be due to give slave labor. Indeed, I argue, no person was due to give slave labor!

The supposed Constitutional Authority of paragraph 3 is no such thing. It dissolves into:

(a) an assumption that State laws perpetuating enslavement can be consistent with the 1791 US Constitution (i.e. specifically including The Apportionment Clause and paragraph 1 of Article IV, and Articles IV and V of The Bill of Rights. Yet these are inconsistent with The Fugitive Slave Clause. Hence it had no Constitutional authority – though in the Constitutions);

(b) a view that (US) people enslaved must be 'owned' as slaves of 'a party', because State law(s) (unjustly) treat them as having no personal liberty [or (Federal) rights!] This ignores the fact that under Federal Law they might logically be construed as presently 'unfree' not lifelong slaves! Also no Federal check or (even) restraint was always carried out on any 'party' (or his 'agents') (to see if they were liars).

Note that these points arise from facts about the 1788 and 1791 Federal Constitutions – so should never be overturned by Courts (either Federal or State) despite *Marbury v. Madison*. For was this an accurate reading of the 1791 US Constitution?

So both assumptions, (a) and (b), are false.

Incidentally, the Supreme Court itself failed gravely to give an accurate and dispassionate reading of the 1791 Federal Constitution at least three times. First when it held that The Bill of Rights Articles did not bind US States – an odd and invalid view since, if that was the case, the 1791 US Constitution was not 'the Supreme Law of the USA' – which it most explicitly declared it was.

The second case was the notorious *Dred Scott v. Sandford* case when Chief Justice Taney took it upon himself to say that a negro could not be – or have been – a US citizen. This falsehood – which had no intelligible relation to the 1788 or 1791 Constitution – was based on biased and inadequately researched history. It had no basis whatever in either Constitutions! (No wonder some of Taney's fellow Justices did not agree!)

The third case was when Prigg's Case was appealed to the Supreme Court – which then implied The Bill of Rights was for 'whites' only! (which was both false and invidious).

Chapter 22

It will be argued (against my reasoning) that the crux of The Fugitive Slave Clause is that some persons are held to 'service or labor' under the laws of US States (e.g. South Carolina or Virginia or Arkansas). It is then argued such people were slaves – since State laws held them as such. Further State laws could – and did bind slaves to that condition. They were legally bound to (forced) work to a 'party' – who – it is said 'owned' them.

Such a line of thought ignores a far more central point. That a person may be classed as a slave in and by a US State but contrary to the Federal Constitution – which is 'the Supreme Law of the USA'. For Article I of the Constitution – a section of which is The Apportionment Clause – requires that Representation of the US people in the lower House of Congress necessarily depends on enumerating many 'unfree persons' as individuals – at least as enumerated persons. It follows logically and directly that any State which treats such persons as chattel slaves may be interfering with the count – since 'owners' can withhold them (at will). Hence that State violates the 1791 Constitution.

Any appearance of paradox or weak, invalid, reasoning in this latter point is quickly dispelled due to these facts:

(a) the word 'held' (i.e. to service or labor), is very much weaker and less binding than words used of free labor in 'The Apportionment Clause' (Article I, a paragraph of Section 2), of both US Constitutions!! There the words are – 'bound to labor'! How can people 'held' to labor or service be lesser persons of lesser account than people 'bound to labor'? How can they be treated as chattels when Congress could not function unless they were enumerated as people?

(b) This fact leaps out from the texts to all who read first

'The Apportionment Clause' and then the so–called 'Fugitive Slave Clause'. Therefore it is (very) reasonable to believe, initially, that the 'Fugitive Slave Clause' will be about free labor or service (under a State's laws) and 'escape' from that. Not about 'escape' from life-long forced labor secured by violence! The Constitution – quite deliberately – does not use 'bound to labor' in The Fugitive Slave Clause. So it indicates that State laws may not claim to bind anyone to forced labor.

(c) Therefore also it is reasonable to hold the position that the 'escaped' person was not bound to US 'State slavery' – which usually meant life-long forced labor and captivity (by owner and State) – but only to some term of labor or service. Some 'Southern' slaves were emancipated – but neither States nor owners looked on this as part of slave status! They thought – quite wrongly – that that was a category even under Constitutional Law.

The owner and the State would deny this point. But the onus of proof is on them to slow there is always a real possibility of emancipation. If they cannot do this – and there was no such possibility for most slaves in 'Slave States'! – then the claim of the 'party' is, I argue, Unconstitutional. For three reasons:

(1) It allows a State to interpret both Constitutions arbitrarily;
(2) slaves cannot always be enumerated even by State (still less by Federal officials but this is required by Article I – for Apportionment) at least in the sense that the count could possibly be checked by Federal officials;
(3) they are liable to illegal treatment (in some States). They are also liable to be maimed or even killed. And as we know some did 'escape'. Hence were not counted.

Yet these arrangements occurred in States of the USA. So it follows logically that:

(i) chattel slavery
(ii) 'owners punishments – at will'

(iii) State classification of some persons as 'owned'

(iv) The Fugitive Slave Clause

were all – though allowed in Customary Law – unsafe and inconsistent with the 1791 Supreme Law of the United States.

Chapter 23

A critic (of my case) will again reply: "you are ignoring the 'legal binding force' of US State laws".

I answer: "No! The onus is on you, the critic, to show that State laws enforcing captivity and life-long forced labor have any standing in 'the Supreme Law of the United States', which is explicitly defined – in part – as the (1788 and then – even more final – the 1791) United States Constitution". And so it includes The Bill of Rights!

The Abolitionists – rightly – pointed out that all slavery was – always – unjust and had never, as far as is known, involved 'due process of law'! These points will be vital ones, but at this stage it is not necessary to use them. We can simply ask the critic:

(A) Since both Constitutions were ordained by the people of the United States and explicitly said to concern (also) 'their posterity' – how can forced labor of millions for an indefinite time-span, and set up by State laws, aid 'domestic tranquillity' – a stated aim of both Constitutions? Or 'Liberty? Or Justice?

One does not need any special or economic education to see that a violently enforced and controlled pyramid of exploitation of (in this case), people unjustly enslaved may explode in the faces of the posterity of people of the USA. Indeed it may do so several times. There will be a tendency when it has happened once for slave-owners to use (even) more violence (than previously – and that was pervasive violence – at all stages in each 'Slave' State).

Also I ask the critic:

(B) How do you know that either the Common Law or the 1791 US Constitution sanctioned any State slave laws? How do you know that such laws could even be expressed either in

Common Law or Constitutional Law? (Granted State Laws may not have been expressed as exactly as Federal Law was – but they had to be in accord with it.)

Lord Chief Justice Mansfield had already decided in 1772 – in the James Somerset case – that slavery was not recognised by English Common Law. [Unfortunately he added that slavery was so odious that it could only be 'justified' by 'positive law'. (He cannot have meant 'morally justified' – so his point comes to saying that slavery accords with some law(s) in some legal jurisdictions – but cannot accord with English Common Law.)]

These two points of his cut both ways in the United States as of 1788 to 1791. Was 'the Common Law' as applicable in the early United States English Common Law? Presumably not. The 'Common Law' tradition (or should one say traditions) had allowed (many) other precedents than English ones. On the other hand was it so divergent that chattel slavery as such was not also 'odious' in Common Law in the United States? Note that close imprisonment for a long period was regarded by most Americans as 'odious' and also demeaning. Imprisonment of the innocent is regarded by all Americans as shameful. But US State slavery usually was life-long captivity of the innocent. So was slavery in US Common Law hateful ('odious')? State Judges took it as 'odious' that an innocent person should suffer life-long imprisonment in the United States! And, as far as is known, US slaves were when enslaved innocent of (any) crime.

There would be a counter-argument of US slave-holders. They would argue US chattel slavery was an Institution allowed for hundreds of years, (at least from 1630), in (some) American Colonies and then in (some) American States. They would say it was law in some States and that it was not called 'odious' even in the New Testament, nor regarded as 'odious' by (most) American lawyers or Judges (at least before 1840). How then could it be contrary to Common Law – which must be law as developed in (e.g. Southern) States – let alone so 'odious' as to be hateful?

I answer that this argument proves that people and Courts tolerate, and even encourage, customs which on close inspection are wrong. When closely investigated they do 'war against' Common Law truths. I would point out that even as generally Conservative a rich land-owner as Washington – a member of Virginia's House of Burgesses and given to acquiring even more land – regarded slavery, as leading directly to a 'tame and abject' servile condition of 'the blacks' over whom he exercised arbitrary sway! Is not this an open admission that US slavery was very harmful? Even so prejudiced a Judge as Chief Justice Taney explicitly allowed – in *Dred Scott v. Sandford* – that 'blacks' were sometimes State citizens. Even from Taney's inaccurate history and biased reasoning it would follow that 'blacks' as such were not 'tame and abject' since some were active State citizens. So it was slavery that made them (in Washington's words) 'tame and abject' though not of course all of them since some were not. Some historians – for instance John Anthony Scott in *Hard Trials on My Way* (Mentor Books, 1974, chapters 3–6) argue that many resisted slavery and owner and overseer power at great sufferings to themselves.

Taney's reasoning from the premise that 'blacks' had in the early (and later) USA never been regarded as having the ability to maintain US citizenship did lead to a contradiction – since many 'white' US citizens showed less activity in that status then, for instance, some 'blacks' – the most famous being Frederick Douglass – who worked their way (by escape from slavery) then work and education to leading positions in the USA. Douglass, for instance, was asked to talk with President Lincoln on major issues – e.g. problems and future of the United States. So Lincoln must have thought him as capable (of US citizenship) as many 'whites'.

Chapter 24

The Fugitive Slave Clause was technically and literally in the (1788 and 1791) US Constitutions. As generally interpreted it meant that 'claims' of a 'party' could be actively taken forward by him or even his agents. Hence from (late) 1788 even 'free blacks' could be hunted as slaves – though they were not slaves. But this was a violation of the 1791 US Constitution. Hence there must have been something Unconstitutional about The Fugitive Slave Clause as generally interpreted!

The slavery of free blacks was 'odious'. The slavery of all 'blacks' was shameful – they were innocent (of crime in particular). Further since American Common Law used ideas of liberty of the innocent (not guilty of, or even accused of, crime) was there not some argument that (all) 'Negro Slavery' was odious by and in a part of American Common Law (though possibly not in other parts)?

The 1791 US Constitution implied (I argue), by appeal to (developed) 'Common Law' ideas of rights and liberties that slavery was 'odious' as it excluded rights and liberties! (Odious but 'Customary Law'.) So how could 'full faith and credit' be given to State laws which (in fact) made people forced laborers and captives – and so 'slaves' in a State and of an owner? There was a latent contradiction in these positions. Note 'full faith and credit' was also to be given (in all States) to the 'judicial acts' of Free States! This again implies The Fugitive Slave Act as it worked was – clearly – unconstitutional.

We have seen that the word 'slave' is and was entirely absent from both Constitutions (1788 and 1791)! Why? I think a reason may have been that the Framers (e.g. James Madison), knew slavery was wrong but they had become habituated to very much slavery existing in the USA – and knew that Congress would wish it 'allowed' as a (so-called) 'Southern Institution'.

On the other hand it may also be true that many US lawyers – including very experienced and distinguished ones – would have concentrated on Lord Mansfield's second point – and argued that US slavery was 'justified' by the 'positive law' of some States. (Some held the ridiculous view that US slavery was morally justified.) They might also have said US States' laws were 'positive law'.

Chapter 25

However the phrasing of the 'Fugitive Slave Clause' is ambiguous. Note first the very treacherous word, 'claim', which may be understood in at least five ways:

(1) an allegation (only);
(2) an assertion which either is or appears to be backed by some evidence;
(3) an assertion made on some evidence which can be checked;
(4) an assertion made on strong evidence (but much time might be needed to check whether the evidence is conclusive);
(5) a provable assertion – proved on and from evidence – (a) legal, (b) historical, or even (c) only logical reasoning, (or a mix of all three).

A 'claim' might only be a case of an allegation – though other 'claims' could range from (1) to (4) – or even (5). The deceit in the clause is concealed from sight – and the word 'party' is used as if the claimant had presented his assertion to a Court or Judge. Note the claimant was not required to have proved a title or even his (or her) claim. He might be an 'owner' according to his State. So what?

It was true that for many years – from 1788 to at least 1850 – and some scholars might argue till 1860 – the influence of Southern views on Constitutional interpretation was very strong. This was true of the Supreme Court itself. Three times (at least) it implied that 'black slaves' were not entitled to the rights in The Bill of Rights (for instance in Dred Scott's Appeal and in the appeal on Prigg's Case).

Is it possible then to sustain (and take forward) the argument Alvan Stewart (and I) give(s) that Federal Law gave the rights in at least Article V of The Bill of Rights to slaves?

Yes – because:

(1) The Supreme Court made demonstrable historical, and conceptual mistakes on these occasions. 'Persons' in The Bill of Rights cannot mean only 'whites'! 'Blacks' could have been Federal citizens! These are facts the Court got wrong.

(2) As Lincoln said Supreme Court decisions might not forever stand as they were (then) on major issues.

(3) Federal Law had a latent power not always seen (even by a Federal Government when dominated by 'Southern' ideas).

(4) The US Congress had sponsored what was said in The Declaration of Independence. Also, The Bill of Rights was in the US 'Supreme Law'. Lincoln made another great argument:

(5) The USA had had – and did have – an Organic Law.

Chapter 26

Before exploring the Organic Law note that as time went on some States began to recognise, and decided to stop, the kidnapping of 'free blacks'. The scope and (usually violent) 'powers' of slave-hunters' unleashed by The Fugitive Slave Clause were there illegal. (Note again the deceit in the clause. No powers are specified! Yet the fugitive (slave) must be 'delivered-up' – hence 'slave-hunters' can appear in a State, (e.g. Massachusetts, Pennsylvania, New York), prepared to violently capture a presumed slave (who is said to be a fugitive slave) but he or she is legally free (e.g. a 'free black')). Pennsylvania decided to – and did – pass as Act of 1826 to prevent kidnap. (As John Anthony Scott says – on page 170 of *Hard Trials on My Way* – this Act did not guarantee a slave the right to a fair trial – but it did make it an indictable criminal offense to kidnap and 'deliver up' to another State a 'free black'). New York and Vermont – both in 1840 – followed Pennsylvania in this. (Incidentally Maryland, which in some respects had been less hard-line pro-slavery at all costs than other States in the South had provoked Pennsylvania's action since Maryland slave-hunters had been very active in Pennsylvania.) The case of a slave, Margaret Morgan, who fled from Maryland to Pennsylvania in 1832 – but in 1837 was seized by an agent, Edward Prigg and was (illegally under Pennsylvania law) returned to Maryland, resulted in the arrest of Prigg when he returned to Pennsylvania.

This case was then appealed to The Supreme Court. The Court – ignoring not only Mrs Morgan's rights, the 1791 Constitution – taken as a whole – with The Bill of Rights – and also the national interests of the USA to justice and peace – incredibly, decided that there was an absolute, national, non-defeasible right to property in slaves. (Thus it implied a negation at one stroke of both The Declaration of Independence which claimed freedom as a birth right of all men [here 'persons' should have been the word and concept Jefferson used] and The Bill of Rights!)

The Court held the 1826 Pennsylvania Act was void and that there was an additional national 'right' (power was what it alluded to!) to recapture fugitive slaves – even calling this 'anew and positive right'!) But how could it be new if:

(a) There was already a so-called Fugitive Slave Clause; and
(b) A slave in a 'Free State' was a slave? (which I deny and also deny 'unfree persons' were necessarily slaves!)?

Chapter 27

Lincoln argued that every real (National) State has an 'Organic Law'. He seems to have thought this existed (in the USA) before the (1788) Constitution. I think Lincoln's general point may have been that every Nation, that attains to some self-understanding and (in due course) written laws, embodies some Constitutive Idea which can be expressed, and which can – and does – become shared (to some extent) by people who think of themselves as belonging to that Nation.

If this interpretation of Lincoln is on the right lines then, I think, he called this 'Idea' an Organic Law because it was the focus (initially) of the Nation's growth. Was there then in the United States from 1765, [a year when many became dissatisfied with British 'authority', (not all by any means)], to 1788, any focus of Independent National growth? I think there was . . . I may not be wholly right in identifying it but it would seem to consist of three main points:

(1) Government(s) derive (some just) powers only from the consent of the governed (i.e. the US people). (Jefferson – in The Declaration of Independence.). Also taxes should be by consent of 'the people'.

(2) In the USA (the States – later also the Territories), government is to be 'of the people, for the people, by the people'. (As Lincoln later phrase this great concept in his Address at Gettysburg.)

(3) 'In America the law is King'. More exactly (from Independence) there is to be no King except (in a metaphorical sense), the 'Supreme Law of the USA' and laws made under its authority. This I take to be what (most) US citizens made of Tom Paine's slogan – at least the many interested in domestic politics. (Paine's statement was made before US Independence.)

Each of these three great points was capable of development – logically and practically. I now argue that, if they constituted much of the 'Organic Law' of the USA, such development in each case was antithetical to indefinite US slavery. (I grant that both Customary Law(s) and some Constitutional interpretation made for a time State slavery a fact of life.)

Lincoln's idea of the Organic Law of the USA was much more revolutionary than his interpretation of the US Constitutions of 1788 and 1791. Though he may have seen these as heralds or even proclamations of liberty there was:

(a) no guarantee of actual freedom of slaves until at earliest 1863 (even then only some slaves);

(b) no guarantee that Articles IV and V of Bill of Rights would be applied to make slaves generally free.

Lincoln's reverence for the 1788 and 1791 US Constitutions is fully understandable since he read them as great documents written by great champions of American freedom. He probably also thought of this as American liberty. If freedom is not identical with social liberty then 'free blacks' might not have had social liberty.

American social liberty would at least imply social freedoms of marriage, residence, work, movement, assembly) for all American permanent inhabitants. This did not exist in Lincoln's time – and, as The US Civil Rights movement proves, did not even exist when Martin Luther King died – though he, Robert Kennedy and Lyndon Johnson did substantially bring it about. (As the Mildred Loving Case proves freedom to marry whom you choose was routinely denied (for instance to 'black' people) by actions of local officials – (in her case a sheriff) – up to the late 1950s. She had to take her 'case' to the Supreme Court.)

Chapter 28

I have already indicated how the US Supreme Law would be antithetical to indefinite slavery in the USA. Article IV of both Constitutions concerns arrangements between States – not any grant of legislative powers by the people! No legislative power permitting continued enslavement has – I argue – ever been granted by the people of the USA – (in that Section, (I), of each Constitution concerning grants of legislative powers)! And the 'Fugitive Slave Clause' does not simply say 'slaves' are to be resident with their 'owners' – which possibly would concern relations of US States – it says they must be 'delivered up' to individual claimants! to any 'party' whose claim is believed valid by e.g. a Magistrate or even just his own State! This sets 'Free States' in conflict with 'parties' who want forcible 'delivery' of slaves back to bondage.

Points (1) and (3) of the Organic Law when logically developed also work against slavery. No consent of any kind was given to slavery by slaves. Nor – very important – by very many free Americans! And The Bill of Rights is part of the US Supreme Law: the Supreme and overriding law above all State laws! And striking down some! 'Slave' States would – of course – argue it did not strike down their 'slave laws' – but this is an assertion not an argument – and examination of The Bill of Rights will show it is a false assertion.

So if Lincoln is right and there was an Organic Law of the US and if it contains any of the three points I gave it works to exclude slavery from the US – firstly by conceptual reasoning and secondly, (after this has been noticed), by practical measures – both relating to Constitutional Amendments and the powers granted to Congress and the President. (Perhaps also by restricting Constitutional Interpretation: e.g. it would rule out *Dred Scott v. Sandford* as a Constitutional Interpretation by the Supreme Court – by showing it was inconsistent with point (1) of the 'Organic Law'.)

Chapter 29

It will be said my statements are Utopian. The 'Organic Law' was recognised by Lincoln – but who else? Did not Chief Justice Taney's judgment in The Dred Scott case allow slavery? Yet some unfree 'negroes' were counted (enumerated) for representation of the US people – all were persons – some had been citizens – and must be (by both Constitutions – (see The Preamble) objects of US justice! The US people could not achieve justice unless they were fair to (all) such persons. (Taney's history was assumed, not researched.) Even a man so rich as Washington, had eighty years before the US Civil War, seen that US slavery was of its nature arbitrary, demeaning and so unjust.

The Supreme Court's attention to the 1791 US Constitution (in Dred Scott!) was both biased and – in at least three cases – superficial. But if the Court was wrong were not Presidents in favour of slavery? Some were. But this proves, at most, that they believed US slavery and States' rights were as *Barron v. Baltimore,* implied (i.e. States were not 'under' The Bill of Rights. But they were, for – as Alvan Stewart held – no US slave had been deprived of his or liberty after a jury trial!) Article V of The Bill of Rights states no person may be deprived of liberty (save criminals). All slaves had been deprived of liberty – so their liberty should be given them in the USA. The Court was wrong in holding persons specifically given Constitutional rights could not assert them in and against the States. But though wrong the Court had the authority to say this and make that de facto law (then and until a later Supreme Court judged exactly contrary to the earlier 'mistake').

So it was important, as well as right in theory, to say that no US State slavery was consistent with the 1791 US Constitution! Constitutionally guaranteed US rights hold even though US Courts or Presidents deny them or States!

Chapter 30

(1) The 1775 Declaration of Independence had said that all men, because of their being created have an unalienable right to liberty.

This clearly means – 'all people' – otherwise Jefferson would have to have given (invalid) reasoning that women were not 'created'! Or 'created equal'.

An unalienable right (given to a person by the Creator by virtue of His act of creation), is logically prior to and remains in force whatever States' rights are. If they deprive a person of liberty they are 'invalid' in the sense that the unalienable right remains and overrides them. (Jefferson had made little explicit distinction between freedom and social liberty.)

(2) The Declaration had been issued by Congress. So a main aim of the Union was to secure people a right to freedom!

(3) Had any right – executive, legislative or judicial – been given by 'people of the ' to enslave persons?

(4) Could a state bind someone to service or labor permanently? (If someone argues that such a right derives from the practice of US slavery, then the answer is – 'That is a practice only'.) In any case how could US citizens mandate permanent enslavement if they aimed at justice (and liberty)?

(5) 'Parties' in any State which claimed 'slaves' under State laws (and under The Fugitive Slave Clause – and the Act of 1793), would have to show – in theory – (though not usually in practice) – they were not breaking The Bill of Rights. How could they prove this when Article V of The Bill forbade such a practice?

For these reasons and because, for instance, the slave-hunters neither observed The Bill of Rights nor acted peacefully, the

'Fugitive Slave Clause' (and the 1793 Act), were causes of both breaches of peace and violent cruelty. So the clause was against both the US Organic Law and the US Constitutions (both of 1788 and 1791)! [Recall that it worked against 'Apportionment' (of Article I of each US Constitution.)]

Some scholars argue slaves were not 'people of the USA'. This may be technically correct as of 1791. Yet all slaves were:

(i)   State residents;
(ii) under State laws;
(iii) by the 'Fugitive Slave Clause' intended to be permanent residents of the State of their 'owner';
      So they were among the people of US States!
(iv) 'under Federal Law' – at least to the extent that they were not allowed to break it and some Articles were held to apply to them; and
(v)   neither foreigners nor aliens nor rebels.

Granted they were not US Citizens – but in view of all of (i) – (v) this may be a minor and not decisive consideration. For could persons with an inalienable right to liberty be 'by State right' slaves? No – only de facto not de jure! This is shown by the case of Elizabeth Freeman. She won her freedom in Massachusetts, appealing to its Declaration of Rights – inalienable rights)! (One such was added to Jefferson's list – the right to be a free citizen of the State.)

It is also doubtful if the 'Apportionment Clause' could operate at all unless (most) unfree people could assemble. (Some were in fact slaves.) In any case many 'unfree' people (i.e. slaves) counted for Representation of the People.

Further, by Article I of The Bill of Rights, the people [at least in peacetime (though there is no such verbal restriction)], have a right (a legal claim which even Congress may not stop) to petition the Government for a redress of grievances! But could Abolitionists assemble to petition the Government – for a redress of slave grievances? Assembly is one of the 'rights of the people'. It may or may not be true that only US citizens are construed as 'the people'. But even then, US citizens have a right to petition the Federal Government for a redress of slavery!! Notice carefully this is a Constitutional right – so overrides State objections. Yet they were not allowed this right in most 'Slave States'.

So the 'general' view that 'the people' did not include slaves is here not relevant. The 'consensus' view does explain some facts of US history and law in 1788 it increasingly fails to explain many facts of US history from (as early as) 1810 on. (The full force of The Bill of Rights rook time to be appreciated – and was not appreciated early.)

Hence it may be reasonable – though not proven – to hold a more nuanced view of what 'We, the people of the United States' came to mean – even if it did not initially mean that in 1788.

Chapter 31

Washington as a statesman should have considered emancipation in relation to one clear aim of the US Independence cause – Freedom for Americans leading to some social equality greater than in a monarchical or aristocratic society. (This was later an aim dear to Lincoln's heart.)

Franklin and Jefferson (and later Lincoln, Seward, Chase and Grant – and probably also the fair-minded Robert E. Lee) grasped this point. Jefferson, for instance, contributed largely to a very liberal new Constitution for Virginia. And, as President Washington did see clearly that social dissension endangered even the (1791) Constitution. But did he fully grasp Jefferson's proposition (in The Declaration of Independence) that all men were created equal? And they had rights to (among other things) life, work, liberty and marriage? Before 1794 he made statements about US liberty – as if this was merely 'freedom from British direction' (and Kingship). But liberty has a social dimension – it implies a society free of slavery! 'Liberty' was not a word that meant the same as 'freedom from (British) tyranny'. Washington did not use the word 'liberty', with attention to its meaning and connotations. His ignorance even extended to not checking that George III was a champion of liberty!

Perhaps Washington took over the word from the writings of Locke, Adams and Jefferson – or, used it because Americans in the States (and Congress), considered it an important expression to state their aims. Washington's dispositions and psychology were (often) rather 'conservative' and to follow American practice in the use of words was in line with this psychology.

But – as events proved – few 'black' American after 1791 – except some of the well off and lawyers and lawmakers – had much liberty – if he could be (violently arbitrarily) claimed by (slave-hunters) as a slave – and transported to slavery. He or she may have had –

temporary and indefinite – freedom(s) (e.g. freedom to write for the Press and to vote) – but that is not the same thing as social liberty – which involves living in a society where both negative and positive freedoms are respected, recognised and (as far as possible) ensured.

It is true that in many parts of the USA (e.g. Philadelphia), most citizens had the benefits of some liberty. And such classes as officers in the US army were almost always safe from captivity into slavery. But many people were not safe. For instance, free 'blacks' were not. Could this be said to be a society where the people enjoyed liberty? I say: No!

By contrast George III had no slaves, thought slavery wrong, would not have allowed either a continuous slave-trade or slavery to last into the nineteenth century. Washington's sheer lack of empirical knowledge was so great he did not even know his ignorance. In sum – George III was not a tyrant while Washington did act tyrannically in e.g. buying 'choice slaves' and far later signing the 1793 Fugitive Slave Act!

Chapter 32

Robert Harvey points out that in regard to enslavement and slavery Benjamin Franklin took a wholly different course from Washington [(see page 361), paragraphs 1 and 2 of *A Few Bloody Noses,* chapter 22). He renounced owning slaves before the Revolution; publicly became President of an Abolition Society (in Pennsylvania) in 1785; and four years later petitioned Congress for liberty for 'slaves'. Franklin not Washington is the father of US liberty. (The Independence – and in that sense freedom – of the US is conceptually and practically different.) And earlier John Woolman and Benjamin Lay – later Anthony Benezet and Franklin.

But Samuel Adams, who had acted impressively before the Revolution, activating a society in Boston in favour of freeing slaves, let the cause slip away from him. His work for the Abolition of slavery could have, if continued, made an enormous difference for that cause.

As for Jefferson, it is hard to discover if he at once took to heart his own rhetoric when he wrote it – or for some long time afterwards!! If he did understand what he stated and implied, why did he not follow Franklin's example? Why did he not liberate his own slaves, at least by 1780? [He may have liberated one (Sally Hemmings) or a few, later – but there were numbers he did not liberate.]

Jefferson was – after Washington and Franklin – and perhaps Madison – a man who could have had most influence in the United States to affect the way the US Constitutions (of 1788 and 1791) were read by millions in the US. He had high and clear valuation of human liberty. He had been the main drafter of *The Declaration of Independence* and also of the very liberal *Constitution of Virginia.* He became President.

His private correspondence shows that – as years went by and he approached death – the injustice of slavery was vividly present to him. But when he had earlier said: 'I have sworn eternal enmity on the altar of God to every form of tyranny over the mind of man' did it not come to his mind that the enslavement of his own slaves to work at his direction was a form of tyranny over the mind of man and woman?

(Granted they may have been enslaved before he 'owned' them.) But was not his ownership and hence restriction of their physical and mental freedom such a form of tyranny?? No doubt Jefferson's 'sway' was mild – but by his own words it was tyranny.

Jefferson – like some other slave owners – may have treated 'slaves' well, but this did not affect the fact they were 'property'. So they were not free to cross State lines or worship in other States, as well as not free from enforced labor.

Chapter 33

Both John Adams and James Otis Jr condemned slavery. Patrick Henry and James Madison were not exacting to their slaves. Madison freed a slave who had run away from him. Henry, when he was dying, aimed to free his own slaves.

We can, then, acknowledge many good wishes and many acts of enlightened liberation on the part of some of the Founding Fathers. But in view of their prestige and influence and what they could have dome publicly to help to free many – and, if possible, all – slaves in the US – the lack of public action – except for Franklin, Adams and Otis – was tragic. In view of all their protests (e.g. against Britain, the presence of a British army and King George III) in favour of human liberty and against 'slavery' and 'tyranny' it is a tragedy! If they really loved liberty as much as they said it was strange all slaves were not freed! This was a necessary condition of social liberty.

We see the way public opinion can set the scene for lack of initiative and moral courage about causes regarded as taboo. Many politicians thought it not politic to raise a subject so hedged with prejudice and hatred. In any case Congress would not countenance emancipation. But without public change in the power relationships which entrenched exploitation of labor, slavery would remain indefinitely in the USA. Was that what was to be encouraged by 'US liberty'? Clearly not! Washington should and could have recognised publicly that such was the case. Also Patrick Henry, Jefferson, Samuel Adams and John Adams. And if they objected, as they did, to '(British tyranny' what exactly was the forced labor of US slaves extorted (by force) by US 'owners' but tyranny!

A tyrant [by his own actions, or that of his agents (or troops)], (usually forcibly or by fear) deprives people of social (and usually also legal) freedoms – for instance to speak out against his will as expressed in his actions. That is exactly what many US slave-owners did. The practice of slavery encouraged (cruel) punishments. It was a real tyranny – not the supposed 'tyranny' of George III over the American Colonies.

And Slave States were tyrants. That was a tyranny neither King George III nor even Lord North had ever thought of – let alone wished to apply to Americans! (True, Lord North had once said in the House of Commons he would not be content until America was 'prostrate at his feet' – but he was responding – in a very extreme way – to Americans not paying taxes for Colonial Defense. Even Samuel Adams and Patrick Henry would have to allow that an extreme response to that ['American'] behaviour was rational for a British Prime Minister.)

Chapter 34

It is interesting that Lincoln, who never wastes words, in one speech gave a long paragraph with great emphasis to make the point that no-one questioned that Jefferson's *Declaration of Independence* did apply to Negro slaves! If this is true Jefferson himself should have acknowledged it. So we have to take it – which I previously doubted – that Jefferson did understand and take to heart much of his rhetoric. The question then becomes more pressing why he did not act on it? Perhaps he estimated he could not? Was this a factor? Whatever the factors were they prevailed – so that much of Jefferson's writing on freedom was, until 1860, of less use than it should have been for the cause of the emancipation of the slaves!

Had Washington, Jefferson, John Adams, Samuel Adams and Patrick Henry taken public stands against slavery the practice, though still entrenched in the South (and New Jersey!), might have diminished in the North earlier than it did. They would have had to move very prudently and convince many in Congress. Was it not their duty to try – even if only by conditional reasoning: (for instance – 'If slavery persists in the USA indefinitely cruelty and the danger of bloodshed increase. So a time should be set – by law – for its Abolition'.) Had they done so no later Supreme Court could have been as prejudiced as Taney's – or more exactly no Chief Justice who studied – (and did not like Taney assume) – facts.

Lincoln saw the point about The Declaration with great clarity. After 1860 he sometimes argued for it with great force. It is true prejudice was still so great he usually argued for it privately. This cuts both ways. Some may argue that it shows even Washington could have done little effective by public speech. Others may hold that had Washington taken a lead in his time there would not have been so much expressed prejudice – or even concealed prejudice – in Lincoln's time. I hold the second opinion. (Conceding of course that there would still have been great prejudice in favour of slavery.)

Washington as soldier, patriot and General loomed even larger in America's esteem than as President. He could – before his Presidency – have started a movement for emancipation. We have seen that this would have met much opposition in Congress and the South. But its influence would still have been huge. There was the anti-slavery stance of Franklin as a public example. [True, Franklin lived in France (for a time) afterwards.] But that was not on Washington's agenda – even had he not been a future President. There had also been much support for Abolition not only by Quakers (in Philadelphia for instance) but by Baptists. Many Northern States put in place decisive measures for gradual emancipation – but not as early as 1780.

Chapter 35

All slavery is forced captivity. As Jefferson (and Rousseau) stated men are created (Rousseau says 'born') free – that is are free by nature. So not only consciousness and will desire freedom in itself but even human instincts and drives. Moreover, even if freedom were not natural to human will and instinct people are expected to do at least some actions freely. Even slave-drivers and slave-hunters expect people to consent to be indoors at late night. They expect people not to want to be captives. They even expect people to consent to being slaves when this has been forced on them for long time as a habit.

All slavery is inhuman forced labor. This is shown by the fact that the slave cannot (without the owner's permission) change his condition or his or her work. The slave is directed in three senses – to his 'owner's' tasks, whatever his own volition, and to a distinct way of life (or rather death in life) and to punishment – frequent and usually violent. Indeed more violent than most punishments inflicted, except in despotisms or armies or navies in the war.

Each slave is at his or her 'owner's' direction (or that of the 'owner's agent') and is alone in two important human senses:

(a) no-one (except rarely a State itself), can interpose a final barrier to the master's will – even, as Charles Olcott pointed out in early anti-slavery writings, if the 'owner' murder the slave. (Court action later in the USA was not usual in many Southern States, nor even expected nor saved the slave); and

(b) and if the slave did raise an objection to his 'owner's' directions he could be sold in short order, or both whipped and sold.

It follows that (e.g. British and US) slavery was an inhuman lack of a supportive social structure which had legal status and rights.

Consequently many slaves had no psychological security. Most had less than the very poor laborers (who usually had very little). It is true the slave, he or she, could be less prejudiced, status-obsessed, and more mature than the labourer or the owner or his agent. But this counted for nothing in power and legal relations!

Though some owners (e.g. Edward Bates), were benign, many were psychologically status-conscious and power-conscious. (A great many were sadists – see Kenneth Stampp's evidence.) It did not figure to many owners that the slave lived and died by – but not from – exploitative work! The benefit and produce of the work – almost always went to the owner. Only subsistence (or occasionally more), went to the slave. Of course astute owners arranged 'rewards' – some real benefits. But this was not the case for most US slaves (as far as I have read).

The slave was in effect – and by law – a State 'person' but without legal rights, i.e. in effect a State-slave in a Slave Society and State – as well as the chattel of an owner! But this fact also cuts two ways. From the viewpoint of the 'owner' it validated his 'ownership'. But from the viewpoint of the Abolitionist it expressed something rotten in State laws which Federal law ought (and they thought legally could) abolish.

The slaves themselves never had enough leisure or reading matter to study Constitutional points – still less arguments to and fro on Federal law. (A few like Henry Highland Garnett or Frederick Douglass had managed to escape and get an education). But somehow – and particularly from 1840 on – many slaves got a reasoned conviction they had a right to freedom in the USA. And some naturally wished to return to Africa – and freedom there. In both cases they were in the right – and slave-owners (as some realised) ipso facto in the wrong.

A slave had no security in his or her cabin. While this was denied by some slave-owners – and others did respect 'their' slaves living-quarters – there was:

(a) liable to be insecurity, because the owner's will prevailed – the slave could be moved or – far worse – sold;
(b) insecurity because he cabin itself was unsafe – or because a slave's wife could be seduced away from him (in the 'owner's' house).

Incidentally, a slave had no right of access to a clergyman – even to get married! (A 'service' could and would be held by an 'owner' – so historians tell us though it is scarcely believable. Even more wicked a slave's marriage was deliberately devoid of any promise – or assurance or even mention of life-long fidelity. Neither husband or wife was allowed (so to pledge) rights:

Abolitionists had no need to state – as it was so obvious – that a slave had no rights

(A) to state his view of how his work conditions should be improved;
(B) his political opinions;
(C) to consult State laws in official texts or places or to consult a sympathetic clergyman;
(D) to the service of a lawyer (e.g. a barrister in a law court – except by permission of the 'owner' and Court and State. And who would meet the expense unless a lawyer volunteered – which (as far as I know) was rarely allowed in a 'Slave State'?)

Finally – (a point that is vital to empathy with the lack of any social status for slaves [exceptions might be slaves who worked as butlers for the rich and powerful] – or slaves who were employed as 'house slaves' (for instance by State Governors) – though chattel slavery was not 'military' slavery it was in law lower in esteem and status than that! Even the Romans – cruel and heartless to conquered peoples who had defied them, [who they (very often) massacred – and often enslaved if of 'use' to them] – had allowed slaves who were (put as) auxiliary troops to have the possibility of some rank eventually, and possibly emancipation (e.g. after at least twenty years hard and good service). Until the US Civil War there was no such possibility for US slaves! It is just possible a few cases of slaves serving, and then being later treated as 'free blacks', might have happened – as it may have happened in the US War of Independence (without being recorded in most cases).

In sum, the majority of slaves of all ages had no prospect or even possibility of either support or emancipation or status of any sort recognised in law. There were a minority whose owners were humane

– and a minority whose owners did emancipate them. Some States (Maryland, for instance), treated slaves officially at some times with more humanity than others. The 'South' was not always from 1769 to 1780 one monolithic entity dedicated wholly to suppression of slaves by all means and by cruel owners. But crucially all slaves were at the disposal of State and owner power! Kenneth Stampp – a great authority – is right that it was a tragedy for (all) Southerners they did not foresee the full consequences of slavery. But the slaves suffered daily horror and degradation.

In such a state of affairs is it remarkable that many slaves wished to be free, and to 'escape'. Which seemed the only viable chance of freedom? But even the word 'escape' is loaded. As Abolitionists rightly stated slaves were reclaiming their right not evading or 'escaping' a rightful claim on them. Kenneth Stampp vividly portrays the 'false consciousness' which went (e.g. in many Southern States), with customary ownership of slaves – the owners soon began to regard it as blameworthy that their slaves thought of or even wanted to escape!! So a further level of psychological tyranny was added to the slave's condition 'You must be a slave even in your mind'!

M. Sobel has argued that slave music, sociality and values sometimes affected the lives, work, art and values of free people. But that did not affect a slave's status or (generally) conditions (even if it could sometimes have softened his 'owner's' mistreatment of him).

A slave remained a chattel – who could (often) be whipped and (often) sold.

Chapter 36

'Owners' in Southern States claimed that they had a right to the slaves' labor (his forced labor) by State laws – they claimed these were endorsed by the 1788 and 1791 Federal Constitutions. The main place in the Constitutions which seemed to endorse and enforce slavery was The Fugitive Slave Clause.

So let us then look more minutely at the exact position _and_ wording of the (1788 and 1791) 'Fugitive Slave Clause'. It is in Article IV. This appears to concern the position, relations and legal status of States in the Federal Union. In particular it is the third paragraph of Section 2 of that Article – which in full is:

(Section 2)
Paragraph 1
The citizens of each State shall be entitled to all privileges and immunities of citizens in the several States.
Paragraph 2
A _person_ charged in any State with treason, felony or other crimes, who shall flee from _justice_ and be found in another State, shall on demand of the Executive authority of the State from which he fled be delivered up to be removed to the State having jurisdiction of the crime. (My italics)
Paragraph 3
No _person_ held to service or labor in one State under the laws thereof, escaping into another, shall, in consequence of any law or regulation therein, be discharged from such service or labor but shall be delivered up by claim of the party to whom such service or labor may be due. (My italics)

So – as already noted – Paragraph 3 is about persons of a specified class ad description. It is not about any criminals – otherwise it would have been a further section of Paragraph 2 (which is about crimes and criminals). It would have concerned some of the 'other crimes', and they would have been described. Secondly the terms 'escape' and 'delivered up' are used in Paragraph 3. Note that whatever 'escape' means it does not and cannot mean 'flee from justice' which is the word used of fleeing criminals. But in abusive language – which recalls Paragraph 2 – the 'escapee' is to be 'delivered up. (Notice very carefully Paragraph 2 concerns anyone in a State who flees from justice – that is why Paragraph 3 cannot concern them.) Thirdly notice that an 'escaped slave' could be 'discharged from labor' in theory by Federal Law. Fourthly – a far less obvious point, but one that stands out to anyone who has read the Constitution – the question at once raises itself whether the 'escapers' are 'free' men or women?

This point which (as far as I know), historians seldom discuss, is of cardinal importance! The reason (as already noted), is that Article I, (in the Apportionment section), has specifically mentioned 'free persons who are bound to service for a term of years'! A natural assumption to make is that the persons 'held to service (under the laws of a State)' are free persons bound to service (i.e. the free persons of Article I). (Granted Article I does not say they are bound to service 'under the laws of a State'.) Hence (Constitutionally) from 1791 to 1862 – the onus of proving the escaped person not free but a slave, though 'held' (not 'bound'!) to service by a State's laws is at once put on both 'a party' and his (or her) State! As far as I know this point about the Federal Constitution of 1791 was never addressed by a lawyer acting for a slave-owner. But it is exactly the point Constitutional lawyers both should and could have raised.

Why should a person held to service or labor, under State law, not be free? Only because of some feature of State laws. Yet whatever that was the 1791 US Constitution did not describe him (or her) as <u>bound</u> to labor! So since he was not bound to labor in the eyes of Federal Law why should he not change State? More exactly still – since 'the Supreme Law of the USA' specifically does not describe him or her as 'bound to labor' but only 'held to labor . . . ' – and since some free persons are 'bound' to labor, those people – whoever they are – who are 'held to labor . . . under a State's laws' could be free so far as their Constitutional status goes. Indeed both Constitutions describe them as people who may have service or labor 'due' to some 'party' (not called an 'owner' – by quite deliberate choice of Constitutional wording – since 'slave-ownership' is deliberately not mentioned anywhere in either Constitution. Yet, since US slaver was generally thought of as an Institution (in some States), it would have been mentioned there quite naturally had it not been an explosive (and evil topic).

Chapter 37

It was not only The Bill of Rights which prohibited slavery. The North-West Ordinance of 1787 prohibited slavery in Ohio and the Great Lakes Territories. The Ordinance could in theory be changed by Congress – it was not textually Constitutional Law in the way that 'The Fugitive Slave Clause' appeared to be. But it expressed at least an intention of Congress in 1787.

From that time to this, slave-owners and also lawyers, historians and other scholars, often stated that slavery was an institution – and built into the social and economic life of the South. Slave-owners (also) argued that neither Congress nor the North had any right to interfere with this institution especially as it embodied a (natural and legal) right to private property.

But they were wrong! The only relevant sense in which slavery (in the South for instance), was an institution was one that inherently meant it should be eradicated. It was a long-time practice of capturing and claiming human beings. Such long established practice were only institutions in a degenerate sense. (Would anyone call some rich men having mistresses an Institution? No. It is a practice.)

The reason is simple. Slavery was both detrimental and dangerous to society! Institutions – such as marriage, schooling and banks – are (if used for the functions they serve), beneficial to society! Property in human flesh is not beneficial to society and is neither a right not an institution. This point was overlooked by all theorists of slavery I think. (Of course slavery made owners rich: but it degraded them and their society. And their apologists.)

If anyone doubts that slavery was dangerous to American society he has only to inquire into:

(a) the conditions of the slaves;
(b) their treatment and the justified resentment of many;

(c) violence against Abolitionists by supporters of slavery);

(d) violence when slaves were taken into new territories;

(e) the disputes over both Fugitive Slave Acts (1793 and 1850);

(f) 'slave revolts' – and 'slave patrols' and 'slave punishments': all three embody brutal and continued violent suppression, or killing, or bodily harm to the slaves;

(g) US politics to 1860;

(h) violence to a Senator in the Senate (i.e. to Charles Sumner);

(i) the Civil War itself, with a toll of lives that crippled and tortured the United States;

(j) the assassination of Lincoln;

(k) the 'Black Codes';

(l) the birth of the Klu Klux Klan.

The conceptual point that slavery was a dangerous practice (not a beneficial institution), was – and is – very widely overlooked. It was also convenient not to inquire into the social conditions of slaves as a human group – only into the economic effects of their exploited labor. (Some Southern women did so inquire – and were almost always marginalised.)

Moreover even from 1769 on, year by year the conceptual space in which American tyranny could be openly exposed, debated and reformed, shrank. The more the struggle for Independence and liberty was thought of as a struggle against British Monarchical tyranny – and liberty was thought of as freedom for citizens of the States

– and so for US citizens (the two groups being held the same), the less lack of liberty (of other Americans) and the sheer tyranny (over slaves and 'Indians') were thought fit subjects for prolonged and detailed free public discussion by US Citizens and their Representatives.

Chapter 38

Also a necessary condition for 'Independence' and 'liberty' was thought – quite wrongly – to be war (against the British). When US citizens might have been examining relations of power and exploitation generally in North America attention was focused on George III and customs officials (as well as British troops). The main problems of exploitation were evaded completely! A 'false consciousness' pervaded American statesmen – bar Franklin, James Otis, George Mason and others.

Ethnic power relations – since they were conceived of as the agency of 'freemen' (and their associates) against 'racially different groups' were [not universally – but in the centres of political power, (e.g. political parties, State legislatures and Congress)], thought of as subordinate matters for Constitutional adjustment – or, in dangerous conflict situations for armed force. The idea of exploitation by US citizens of other groups was not given its due weight in political discussions and elections. Yet – as history proved (before, during and after the US Civil War) – it was the major problem of the new nation.

The misguided ferocity with which Samuel Adams welcomed a coming war with Britain – which (as Robert Harvey points out) turned out to be a war with huge casualties – meant that he had less time to consider whether any war was a good way forward for Americans. The fact that many Americans wanted a war was not the point of most relevance. That was whether Americans wanted justice.

As things turned out the War of Independence was followed by another war with Britain in 1812, then later by 'the Mexican War'! then later still by the US Civil War! and meanwhile many, so-called, 'Indian Wars'! Some Americans even contemplated a third war with Britain (during the US Civil War)! (Admittedly only a minor one!) American history in the nineteenth century (or at least most of it), was fraught with violence! None of this was inherently necessary – and some of it was due to the idea that to be 'Independent' was to be a warrior.

US development need not have proceeded in this way. It would have been quite possible for a Continental Congress to have:

(a) raised a minimum Defense Tax – and had that ratified by (most) States;

(b) requested all British Army personnel be withdrawn (rather than drawing them into ambushes!), and represented how much Britain would save in expense – and lives! This might not have worked at once – but the financial saving to Britain would have powerfully aided it – and produced results if allied to continuous appeal by respected Americans and their London agents and friends. (Edmund Burke for instance would have agreed and advocated the policy);

(c) made State militias liable for service in an American Defense Force;

(d) stated that they wished to observe either the Proclamation Line or at least any treaties made with 'Indians';

(e) set long-term dates for slave emancipation and settlement with 'Indians'; and

(f) preserved a loose tie with the British Empire – by asking the Crown to visit, say every ten years, and receive reports from Chief Justices to see that American liberties were preserved in the States. (The Crown could have been proclaimed by Congress – 'A Guarantor of American Justice and Freedom'. Even if George III had not wished it could he not have withheld some person [e.g. The Lord Chief Justice of England], to act for the Crown.)

In sum: the US could have had:

(A) peace, not periodic wars;

(B) trade benefits by membership of the Empire (as Roger Harvey says huge trade benefits – though Congress would have had to make clear British mercantilist laws were not viable to Americans);

(C) self-government;

(D) a tie with the British Crown – if and only if the Crown acted as a lawful arbiter so that Americans had freedom to work, move, marry and take part in political and social affairs. No doubt some States would aim to restrict some Americans from freedom (e.g. slaves). The Crown could however have cared for freedoms so visibly that Congress might have acted against slavery (e.g. by 1829).

Chapter 39

The usual and predominant view of scholars of the United States – whether of law, history, institutions, property or military affairs – is that in 1791 until at least 1862 slavery was legal in some States and by Federal Law. But could it be both? Already in 1791 The Bill of Rights at Article V outlawed depriving persons of freedom without due process of law. Slaves were persons! (Also persons of the States.)

And as we have seen:

(a) slaves – if referred to at all in the 1791 Constitution – were 'referred to' as persons;

(b) the great majority – nearly all – Americans in any official (State or Federal) post used this point to say the 1791 Constitution did apply to slaves;

(c) it was false to say that slaves as persons had been deprived of liberty by due process of law – since State laws of slavery were not by due process! They were in fact a contradiction of 'due process of law'!

(d) the only possible defence, then, even of State laws about slavery – since Constitutional law is the Supreme Law of the US and The Bill of Rights 'overrides' State law(s) – is that slaves were not (Constitutionally) 'persons' or that they were, but had not been persons up to 1791.

The first statement is untenable. Firstly it is false! Secondly Article I of the Constitution(s) talks of 'unfree persons'. Nor is it logically available to count a new and 'exclusive' definition of persons in terms of geographical origin! To mention this ruse is to show it is ridiculous – as well as a violation of the history and use of the word 'Person'.

The objector has to fall back on the idea that slaves were not persons before the 1791 Constitution. This is also false. The 1788 US Constitution refers to 'three fifths of all other persons' (i.e. 'unfree' persons for instance)! Hence slaves were Constitutionally persons in (and by) 1788.

It follows logically that neither Constitution restricts the term 'person' to US citizens. So both objections fail. They do not support the view that The Bill of Rights does not extend rights to slaves as persons. Therefore it is unsafe to consider – as of 1791 – Federal law as allowing anyone to be deprived of liberty – (as slaves were) – without due process of law. This conclusion may be denied, but it cannot be refuted. This point is not new – it was seen as early as the late 1830s by the great Abolitionist lawyer, Alvan Stewart. Some of his other insights will come to the fore in further reasoning from The Bill of Rights. Stewart's reasoning – as Jacobus Ten Broek has acknowledged – does not, logically, depend on his Abolitionism. It is:

(A) sheer common sense that slaves had been deprived of liberty!;
(B) were acknowledged Constitutionally, (if mentioned at all! A debatable point), as 'unfree persons';
(C) even one reading of Article V of The Bill of Rights shows that (no) person may be deprived of liberty without due process of law;
(D) due process of law by definition implies a (Court) trial with a jury (save possibly for military traitors – crimes while in the Army, Navy or militia).

Stewart's reasoning is thus clear as crystal – and also rooted in great truths of law and common sense. I am not sure Ten Broek is right to imply such reasoning is daring: but it is compelling and conclusive. No doubt it could be said that the deprivation of liberty often (had) happened before the existence of the United States. True. But so what? If the US Bill of Rights in most direct and explicit terms imaginable states persons may not be deprived of liberty without due process . . . it is neither feasible nor reasonable to imagine the Framers confined this right to only some persons in the US! And slaves were persons in the USA!

Chapter 40

We can apply the conclusion that slaves as persons had a (Constitutional) right not to be deprived of liberty immediately to the 'Fugitive Slave Clause'. How could a person be 'held' to service or labor for life under the laws of a US State when the 1791 Constitution itself (in The Bill of Rights) stated that no person could be deprived of liberty without due process of law? (Article V). By 'liberty' the Constitution must at least mean freedom to move and work to live!

Alvan Stewart held rightly that due process of law implied the right to a jury trial (of not less than twelve and not more than twenty-three! Persons). No State laws on slavery provided that, before a person was declared a slave. Even had they done so what offence would an (innocent) transported 'black' have been guilty of? Hence – ironically – not only were State Lawson slavery unsafe, but The Fugitive Slave Clause itself was, by the Amended (1791) Constitution, contrary to The Bill of Rights – indeed contradictory to it. (Both Articles IV and V of The Bill of Rights, I argue, disallow chattel slavery.)

So – I argue, following the reasoning of Stewart – and contrary to the reasoning of Lincoln – the Fugitive Slave Clause – let alone the later Act of 1793 – was not Constitutional (law) even though in the Constitutional texts. Of course it was 'Customary Law' in the sense people believed it to be law.

There is an opinion of some lawyers and philosophers of law that legal text is always, in the correct contexts, law. So they need an answer in this case. My answer is that the clause was observed by Americans as binding law – but in the light of analysis it was not binding Constitutional law – and being contrary to that was a stipulation which was in fact observed. It was customary law.

The irony is that though it was (as I concede to, for instance, Professor H. L. Hart), positive law it was Constitutionally illegal State

94

laws on life-long slavery were, as we have seen (by Stewart's conclu-sive reasoning), unconstitutional from 1791 (on).

We saw that Lord Chief Justice Mansfield in England in 1772 ruled that slavery was 'so odious' that nothing could justify it except posi-tive law! Perhaps he had in mind the point later made by Professor Hart that existing positive law does not necessarily square with what is right. (He had left a loophole by which US lawyers could argue that slavery was 'according to the 'positive law'(s) of some US States! This was correct. But it was not an argument that slavery was legally allowed by Federal Constitutional Law.)

Chapter 41

We tend to overlook and ignore how well entrenched slavery was in the British North American Colonies in the eighteenth century by the British (e.g. traders selling slaves from Africa to colonists, British Governors allowing slavery and British merchant houses in London which financed ships). William Hague in his *Wilberforce* gives statistics of hundreds of thousands of slaves taken from Africa and forced on to British ships and then sold – to end up in America and the West Indies. (Also hundreds of thousands were also imported to the US from 1775 to 1809).

In New Jersey for instance it was British companies that encouraged in that century a great influx of slaves – already brutalised by 'slave transportation'. Slavery was in many Colonies a pervasive habit, an intensively, continuously cruel practice and an exploitative trade. [It was not – as I have pointed out – an institution beneficial to society – still less (of course) to the wretched people who were enslaved.] Anyone who still thinks slavery (by the British or US) was a useful institution cannot have read the horrors of the slaves (see for instance the middle chapters of Alex Haley's *Roots*. We also tend to forget how relatively tolerant most of the British authorities in British North America were to the (inhuman) practice. State legislatures were let entrench the practice as allowed specifically by 'State positive law(s)'.

This is not to say that colonists were all (even most) in favour of the practice. (This is an area where dogmatism is impossible.) (Perhaps a third became opposed by 1760 to the practice? But this is not recorded (as far as I know). Certainly it is recorded that from then on Quakers, Baptists and Abolitionists were very actively opposed).

G. M. Trevelyan pointed out that those who ignored John Woolman's arguments against enslaving human beings in the eighteenth century left a kind of void which was in the end filled in the nineteenth century by General Grant's army in the Civil War [which became in its middle and especially later stages a fight to allow slaves (e.g. in Southern States such as Virginia) freedom].

John Woolman, Benjamin Lay and Anthony Benezet of Philadelphia, were three very distinguished Quaker leaders and prophets of the anti-slavery cause. In time – as Gary Nash has pointed out – in a kind of seismic shift of opinion whole Quaker meetings and communities were converted to the same cause. Great Revivalist preachers (e.g. Whiteside), also helped to stir people's consciences on the issue in the eighteenth century. Both John Wesley and William Pitt opposed slavery. [An American Tory 'loyalist' pointed out that (some of) the hardest drivers of Negros were most in favour of 'liberty' (so-called I would add).] Nevertheless taken in the whole context of the North American Colonies, anti-slavery progress was at first gradual and then episodic in the eighteenth century.

So even by the time of The Declaration of Independence there was no popular and public consensus that slavery was inherently wicked. There may have been – and probably was – a strong undertow of opinion in many States that the practice was morally wrong – but this did not translate at once by then in most States into changes in law. But in quite a few Northern States (e.g. Rhode Island, New York and Massachusetts and then Connecticut) there was fierce condemnation of slavery – even from 'moderates', and Massachusetts in particular moved against slavery.

Many States did produce new Constitutions (sometimes two), and these did advance the emancipation cause (e.g. by providing for emancipation at later times). But there was no general official state-ment – from Congress – that slavery could not persist in the United States if the US Constitution was to guarantee liberty to persons.

Indeed at some times there was a species of taboo on the subjects of enslavement and slavery [both in Southern States and in Congress. The Slave trade was discussed – sometimes even in Congress. But slavery itself was not widely discussed there (as far as I know).]

And well into the nineteenth century Southern State Governors held that slavery in America was wholly consistent with federal Constitutional freedoms – a view which is false as well as unsafe in law.

Chapter 42

We can now turn to an exact analysis of why the US Bill of Rights of 1791 renders US slavery Unconstitutional. Article I has several prohibitions on Congressional law-making.

<u>Article I: The Bill of Rights</u>
'Congress shall make no law:
(a) respecting an establishment of religion;
(b) or prohibiting the free exercise thereof;
(c) or abridging the freedom of speech or of the Press;
(d) or the right of the people peaceably to assemble; and
(e) to petition the Government for a redress of grievances.' (My italics and lettering)

I concede that they are not absolute in all circumstances! For instance in wartime there could be some constraint on free assembly (to save lives). Note that Congress – the Supreme legislative body in the United States – is not allowed to lay down a religion for the USA. Nor to prohibit the people from exercising religious freedom and practice! It follows that no State legislature should do so. But State legislatures which passed slave laws may have breached the second condition – since an 'owner' might prohibit a slave having religious freedom and especially practice (e.g. time for worship at a church). Even if the 'owner' did not do this he could prevent a slave from religious freedom and practice. For instance by sheer overwork! Notice also that it seems literally true that free worship, free speech, free Press and free assembly may not be prohibited whether or not to free man or to 'unfree' . . . Even if –as most scholars hold – only the free citizens are actually meant as holders of the rights.

Note secondly that – except possibly in time of Rebellion or War (Civil or Foreign), where violence might result from (some) speech or (some) Press articles – Congress shall not abridge free speech or a free Press . . . But officials, mobs, crowds and individuals in 'Slave States' (and in some territories) did so quite regularly, for instance, by murder of Abolitionists or breaking up the Press and premises of anti-slavery journalists, such as James Birney. This was contradictory to the Supreme Law of the USA. In practice (and theory?) Abolitionists and slaves should have been allowed free speech and a free Press. (Save in case of crime or treason.) This was far more in line with the spirit of Article I of The Bill than the (violent) suppression of both groups in some States.

Thirdly, it is the Supreme Law of the USA that the people have a right peaceably to assemble. This implies legal group assembly. Note that slaves were people of the USA – since they were:

(i)   State residents;
(ii) Under State laws;

and by the 'Fugitive Slave Act' intended to be permanent residents of the State of their 'owners'. Even if by 'the people' the Bill only meant to denote US citizens still as a matter of fact slaves were people of the USA. So Abolitionists – who were among 'the people of the USA' – should have exercised their right of assembly without hindrance. And for the cause of slaves.

But Abolitionist protest – and morality and religious expression – was prohibited (illegally) in many Southern States. Hence there was not free speech or a free Press there. Slaves could not petition either State or Federal Government for a redress of grievances for no cruelty by 'slave owners', for no chain-gangs, for no beatings, whippings or murders! Nor was there free movement for 'slaves' and Abolitionists! Nor safety for 'free blacks'. Nor proper education for 'slave' children. And there was forced labor (for slaves). (Even indentured servants [often treated like slaves] by Article I of The Bill of Rights, may have a right to petition even the Federal Government for a redress of grievances.)

We note that Article I of The Bill of Rights visibly treats 'the people' as having (human and legal) rights – and so seems to reinforce the conclusion that can be reached by logical reasoning on the so-called 'Fugitive Slave Clause' that if anyone is free to give 'labor' or 'service', (for a time and under State laws) he or she is not a slave. Even if – as many scholars hold – 'the people' were US citizens still their social freedoms could not be divorced from much slave freedom!

Chapter 43

Article IV of The Bill of Rights concerns – mainly but not by any means wholly –

'the right of the people to be secure in their persons . . . ' (My italics)

Note that a right is asserted to hold (against all 'violation') of 'the people' to security in their persons. This must imply that some persons (e.g. not criminals accused of grave crimes, such as manslaughter or murder or treason), are not to be seized (still less enslaved!) by either the Federal Government, or State Governments, or agencies of either, or individuals.

Even if 'the people' are only US citizens, a question arises as to why personal security, which allows autonomy (at least to a large extent), is important. Two wholly simple answers – related to each other – at once come up:

(a) So that (the) people may be free;
(b) So that (the) people may not be enslaved.

If we now compare these answers to the condition of US slaves the conclusions stare us in the face:

(A) Both US Constitutions, if they mention them at all, do so as persons (admittedly, as 'unfree persons');
(B) These persons are not free – still less have they personal autonomy;
(C) They have been unjustly (and wickedly) enslaved without trial or due legal process.

The questions now arise:

(D) Is this just? Does it benefit the 'slave'? Does it benefit society in the long run?

Or does it corrupt? Does it make peace with other US States less likely (or more)?

(E) Is it in accordance with the spirit of any of Articles 1, 2, 3 and IV of The Bill of Rights? Is it in accord with the letter of Articles IV and V?

The answers to these questions are – with one qualification – 'No'. The only possible qualification is: Suppose some persons – e.g. US citizens – have a right to human property (i.e. the bodies and minds of 'slaves'). This qualification is both inhuman and ridiculous! It is true that many slave-traders and owners stated it. But this does not show it is worth reasonable consideration. Lincoln, for instance, disposed of it conclusively and exhaustively when he asked: What was the reason for slavery? – skin colour was it? 'Then have a care: you may be enslaved by the first man with a whiter skin than your own'? With his striking insight, Lincoln in a few words laid out a conclusive and eternal argument which strikes down any particular ground of slavery – not just skin colour!

It is therefore reasonable, also, to assert that to claim property in human beings is not in accord with the spirit of Article IV – even if it accords with the letter – (which I personally deny). This is because the same reasons, at a ground-zero level which support freedom of citizens, mandate freedom for slaves! For instance:

(i)   humanity;
(ii) sympathy;
(iii) compassion
(iv) social utility;
(v)   religious feeling;
(vi) human fulfillment.

And in an American context: *respect for* **The Declaration of Independence with its account of inalienable human rights.**

(vii)   Logical consistency with The Declaration of Independence.

Anyone who has read The Declaration of Independence with attention – the shorter version approved by Congress, not Jefferson's original – must recognise that it argues not explicitly yet in detail – with several reasons – for freedom for slaves, who are just as much men (and women) as other human beings. (And the longer version – not easily accessible now – has several more reasons.)

For instance, no slave gave consent to (State) slavery – yet Jefferson very specifically states that 'men' may change Government that do not grant them liberty! Jefferson did not, I think, fully state that liberty involves not only personal freedom but social association – but his thoughts directly implies this as a human right. So it logically follows from Jefferson's document that slaves both may, and if they can must, change the Governments of some US States.

So far as I know neither US Constitution defines:

(1) 'free person'
(2) 'unfree person'
(3) 'State citizen'
(4) 'citizen of the USA'

Though Congress can state some points governing naturalisation – and citizenship (I believe) it was an open option for a slave, (if he had ever had a chance at all!), to argue that though he (or she) was at the moment 'unfree', he was so illegally by Federal Law! So he was also (by Federal Law) free.

Of course, a slave who even tried so to argue would, very likely, have been disabled, whipped, and perhaps killed such was the evil of 'the slave-owning power(s)'. But cruelty is not a rational argument – still less is it one that disproves any of the 'slaves' assertions.

Article IV (of The Bill of Rights) only allows very specific conditions for warrants to be issued – which supports the thesis that it is (at least usually) criminals who are to be deprived of freedom. I hold that the spirit of this Article – even if not the letter – supports an American (US) case for freedom for slaves – in line with Jefferson's very much more specific case for slaves having an inalienable right to live in freedom. For the slave was an American person – which he could not

103

be if so deprived of security that he died. It is blindingly obvious that no slave-trader in Africa had ever used an American warrant! Nor I think American slave 'owners' initially on taking the 'slave'! (Nor had British slave traders, shippers, agents and any of the crew of 'slave ships'.)

Chapter 44

Article V of The Bill of Rights was correctly quoted by the great Abolitionist lawyer, Alvan Stewart, as a reason why all US slaves (save criminals), should be freed. The crucial words here (though of course the whole Article should be read), are:

'No person . . . shall be deprived of life, liberty or property without due process of law . . . '

Every US slave – save criminals, [of whom there were some (e.g. Nat Turner) – but note that these had already been unjustly enslaved before their crimes(s)], – had – at the time of his or her first residence (e.g. as a baby), in a US State had been denied (de facto) any legal recourse – against slavery. Yet his liberty was taken illegally.

Stewart rightly drew the conclusion that by Article V of The Bill of Rights all such US slaves were by the Article declared de jure free people! Since Article V was part of the Supreme Law of the United States he rightly concluded they were – or, more exactly, were justly, by an exact reading of the US Supreme Law (which not everyone understood or agreed with), free people in legal status – whatever States or slave-owners thought – or (I conclude) even the Supreme Court!

In one sense, Stewart's point was Utopian – the Supreme Court sometimes vigorously asserted contradictory reasons (e.g. in *Dred Scott v. Sandford*) for most of the 70 years from 1791 to 1861! No 'Slave State' admitted it! Most slave-owners did not! Those slaves who reasoned in a like argument (e.g. Henry Highland Garnett) were vigorously persecuted . . . Those journalists (e.g. James Birney), who favoured 'Abolitionist' reasoning – such as Stewart's – were often assaulted . . . Charles Sumner was nearly clubbed to death (in the Senate!) for asserting slavery was wicked. His injuries were so serious that he was in part immobile – probably paralysed afterwards.

So, what did Stewart's reasoning on Article V of The Bill of Rights achieve? It had considerable effects on Northern public opinion and in some Northern legislatures. Stewart showed that Article V (of The Bill of Rights) was a benchmark which was also a bulwark (against States' misuse of power) – and the benchmark set a standard below which treatment of (non-criminal) American persons may not legally fall.

Historically, treatment usually fall well short of it, for both 'slaves' and 'Indians' – each of them being persecuted. But this did not alter the legal case, as the most far-seeing lawyers of the time, Salmon Chase, William Seward and various of Stewart's associates in 'Abolitionism', came to hold after him.

All save one of the other provisions of Article V (of The Bill of Rights) relate to restraint on the way either Court or 'criminal' proce-dure is to be restricted legally. The sole exception is public use of private property – and this is a place where I can finally dispose of the plausible suggestion that American slaves should ever have been regarded, as *private property*. (I italicise the last two words separately, as overlapping concepts are involved!)

One of the main – probably the main – features which renders property beneficial, is that it can be, and is, used to aid people (to eat, work, play, sleep for instance). This use is (standardly) of things that cannot reply (though today some machines can).

Anyone who thinks human beings are things that can be used without reply, shows he has no understanding – or a perverted one – of the human species.

Anyone who thinks forcible private use of human beings aids human society for human happiness, shows he understands neither –

(a) happiness

nor even

(b) human society as a humane – not merely animal – association.

So much for the unfortunate, long-term myth that private prop-erty in humans is ever a good, or an humane 'Institution'. The long-established classification of US slavery as 'the peculiar Institution' was always odd. It should be (and have been) called an inhuman prac-tice. So much should forever have disposed of slavery, even in America, had Franklin's and Jefferson's ideas been exhaustively studied

– as they should have been! Washington's signing of The Fugitive Slave Act should have been regarded as shameful! (To present it to a President for signing was likewise shameful.)

Article V (of The Bill of Rights) should also have served as a decisive barrier, in both natural and (US) legal justice, against the condition of slavery in the United States, from 1791 on. That it did not do so is an indictment of (many) State Courts and also of many Federal Courts. It is also strange that not all Constitutional scholars related the liberty of persons spoken of in Article V (of The Bill of Rights) to all the 'unfree persons'. [The Apportionment Clause (in Article I of the US Constitution).] But custom, habit and power all mould the interpretation of law, even when this is wrong.

Human blindness thus allowed evil power of the slave-owners to continue. Yet US slavery as such was as I have shown – demonstrably incompatible with the 1791 Bill of Rights itself. So with the US Supreme Law from 1791!

Chapter 45

Questions of meaning support (and underlie) the case that US chattel slavery was from 1791, a breach of Articles IV and V of The Bill of Rights. For if the simple word 'person' changed in meaning from Article I of the (1788 and 1791) Constitutions to (The Articles of) The Bill of Rights, then the Federal Constitution was ambiguous! The Supreme Court, which had authority as a Supreme Judicial body, could not change the US Constitution.

Also, if the word 'person' had varied in its sense then did the words 'free . . . ' and 'unfree . . . ' also vary? Both of them! What about such terms as US State citizen – and US citizen? No – the US Constitution (of 1791) was not a rag-bag of dissonant meanings for key words . . . That is also one reason why 'labor' and 'service' cannot be used to denote 'chattel slavery'. True – 'free person' sometimes connoted 'US Citizen' – but this was 'never' its meaning! Even in law freedom did not necessarily imply US citizenship.

I do not go so far as (I believe) Professor Ronald Dworkin does, in interpreting the 1791 Constitution as a moral document: I think it held some moral values fully but did not see many others – (for instance, protection of the weakest and also of the powerless). I do however go slightly further than most 'Abolitionists' did, in (now) affirming that all permanent residents of the United States – including 'Indians' – should legally have been recognised as entitled to the protection of Articles IV and V of The Bill of Rights. This point is independent of the overwhelming – and unanswerable – case for the freedom of all 'slaves' because of their God-given human created nature and dignity – which was made by the great Quakers – John Woolman, Benjamin Lay and Anthony Benezet (of Philadelphia) – and others, recorded by historians. And was in or implied in Jefferson's thought.

I maintain that the US Bill of Rights gave (some) rights – that to freedom, for instance – to rich and poor, men and women, citizens and 'slaves' (also probably to individual human beings permanently resident in the USA, of whatever colour – and so to Native Americans as well! I grant this is not readily seen – and that it rests mainly on a section of Article V (only) – other Articles just setting a context for Article V).

By no means do I say that this interpretation has been proved beyond doubt . . . But I do affirm that it is both a sound and a feasible interpretation, which makes sense both of the 1791 Constitution as a lasting National Constitution and of the whole history of Constitutional Amendments up to today – which, I argue, do not reject the 1791 Constitution, but attempt to put in much clearer light and focus its bearing on the National Life of the United States. They bring out liberties consistent with but not expressed in, the original Document. Hence I must – and I do – maintain that 'The Fugitive Slave Clause' was not a valid Constitutional prescription.

The Clause

(1) was botched, open–ended, abusive; and
(2) did not bear the sense given it (by lawyers); and
(3) was always wholly Unconstitutional! – since it made The Apportionment Clause in theory unworkable.

I grant this is a paradox . . . But, as T. S. Eliot said, history has many cunning passages!

Chapter 46

One major point. The great logician Kurt Godel was – we are told – chary of taking an oath to become a US citizen because he thought the US Constitution contained an inconsistency. And so a contradiction. Despite (many) Constitutional Amendments (the 13th being Key in this context) the text Godel studied may have been the 1791 one we have met frequently (as it is the one that declares (of itself) it is the Supreme Law of the USA). (Alternatively, Godel may have had some text without the Fugitive Slave Clause – though, I believe, only if Constitutional Amendments after 1791 were added).

If Godel had the full 1791 text then I think:

(1) he would have seen that The Apportionment Clause (in Article I) was not consistent with the slavery – and with 'escaped slaves' – believed to be referred to in the Fugitive Slave Clause. [For instance, how could escaped slaves be enumerated (in the wrong State!) as 'unfree persons'?]; and

(2) he would also have seen – as Alvan Stewart did – that Article V of The Bill of Rights does not allow US slavery – so the Fugitive Slave Clause cannot be valid (i.e. as it was generally interpreted)!; and

(3) he would also have seen that the general account of Fugitive Slave Clause was contradictory to all aims of the Constitution (in The Preamble); and

(4) also he would have asked how could paragraphs 1 and 3 of Article IV of the US Constitution work together.

And how could the abolition of slavery – perhaps gradual but still legal – in some States allow the 'delivering up' of slaves to 'parties' in other States? I doubt if Godel would have held with Lincoln (at parts of his career) that lawyers had some 'Constitutional backing' in acting for 'parties' who claimed slaves.

He may not have agreed with my direct dismissal of all State laws for 'slaves' as outlawed by The Bill of Rights – but it is (I hold) likely he would have agreed with me that 'unfree persons' were not Constitutionally of necessity slaves.

In sum: I can see no grounds he could have recognised US States slavery as valid (under the full US Constitution) of 1791.

Chapter 47

Finally, any lover of liberty must censure both Fugitive Slave Acts – of 1793 and 1850 – as well as The Fugitive Slave Clause. This involves – also – saying frankly that the Presidents who signed them were gravely at fault! Had Franklin's ideas and example been followed, this could never have happened. He – not Washington – is the true father of US social liberty and justice. It is quite ironic that the supposed 'tyrant' George III would never have even dreamed of so curtailing the freedom of anyone (of making them slaves or holding them in and to a 'Slave State'). But Washington did, by signing the 1793 Act. He was both a patriot and a man of good will – but anyone who knows what the 1793 Fugitive Slave Act did, has to admit that in this case Washington was an agent of tyranny – indeed of continued tyranny – since the Act was in force until (at the earliest) 1850 – when another Act was passed! So in practice its idea lasted till 1863.

Can anyone, then, doubt that those who allowed the original Fugitive Slave Clause as Constitutional, made the gravest possible mistake – allowing leeway for later claims that the Acts furthered the aims of the Constitution? Here truly, for all American and other lovers of liberty, was an American tragedy.

It was an American tragedy that could quite simply have been avoided. No such Clause should have been included in the US Constitution(s). On the contrary slavery – of all varieties – should have been banned!

But even as a form of words it was blindingly obvious that no service or labor could be 'due' (from a slave) to a slave-owner, (i.e. any such 'party'), since the slave had been forcibly compelled to a 'slave-life' and had never given consent, or been able to contract or give verbal agreement, to work as a slave. Further: property, (which it was assumed the slave was), cannot be 'due' to give anything: nor can it be 'charged' or 'discharged' – or held or 'forced' to do something (save for property in animals, who are not human). The US Constitution(s) talked of persons – so not of inhuman animals. Nor should even force be applied to such animals!